"It's All About Life"

Love, Dysfunction, Compassion

Harvey E. Lazarus

LAZARUS PUBLISHING

ISBN: 978-0-9964121-0-0
        978-0-9964121-1-7
        978-0-9964121-2-4

Printed in the United States of America by Llumina Press

Library of Congress Control Number: 2015908204

To my son, Gregg.

You will be sorely missed forever.

TABLE OF CONTENTS

Chapter 1

WHERE IT ALL STARTED

On a cold December morning in 1946, my mother took me by the hand on the number 48 bus from Hillside, New Jersey, into Penn Station, Newark. From there we took a train into New York City, followed by a subway ride up to Broadway and the Paramount Building at Forty-Third Street. My mother was an attractive woman of about five foot two inches tall with dark brown hair; she was well dressed and had a determined presence about her.

Although I was totally oblivious to this fact at the age of four, I was about to begin my career as an entrepreneur.

We had come to the office of Saxie Holdsworth, a talent agent recommended by my mother's twin sisters, who believed Saxie had helped further their careers as professional roller skaters. My aunts were convinced I represented the next generation of family talent and was just the right type to pursue a career as a child model.

"Sure," Saxie Holdsworth had told my mother over the phone, "bring him by, and let's see if he has the personality and what it takes to pass the *look* test."

I had no idea what was going on as I stood there before him in his office, but apparently this was not the type of audition that required preparation.

"The kid definitely passes the 'smell' test," Saxie said. "Now what he needs is a professional portfolio of photographs I can submit to modeling jobs that may be available for him."

My mother had made up her mind, and no matter what anyone said, she was going to give this her all. She was seriously committed to this project, regardless of the financial risk involved. She took twenty-five dollars from her savings account—a small fortune for our family in those days—and paid a professional photographer to make a portfolio of me for the agent.

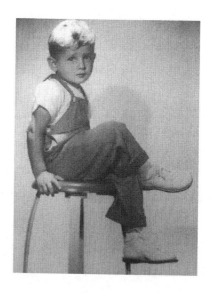

And the investment paid off. At the age of four I was earning fifty dollars an hour (minus the 15 percent Saxie took off the top and the money we had to pay for bus and train fare into New York and subway fare to the photo shoots and interviews). What was left, my mother explained, was going into a savings account she had set up for me to save for my college education. Over the next eight years, my boyish face and physique appeared in many editions of *Radio Mirror* and *True Romance* magazines as well as the *Sears Mail Order Catalogue*. I look at the pictures now and barely recollect the shoots. The one I do remember was the last modeling job I had at the age of twelve for a reversible flannel shirt for a Sears catalogue. I *don't* remember ever seeing the shirt in a single advertisement or in any store, but I do recall it was a nice shirt and I liked it. But they never even let me keep the shirt.

I did like the idea that I was earning money. My brief career as a young teen somehow instilled in me some form of entrepreneurial spirit.

In business for himself, my father was a professional truck driver. He subcontracted to one company, Branch Motor Express. He was very close to the owners of the company. In fact, he'd told me, during the war when they first started, he lent them money to buy license plates for their trucks. He was a very hard worker, but truck-driving only paid so much.

We were a close family—literally as well as figuratively, since there were six of us living in a two-bedroom house in Hillside, New Jersey. One bedroom was used as the master bedroom, and one was used as the den. The attic was converted into two more bedrooms—one for my dad's father, Grandpa Lazarus—and the other was for me and my brother Larry, who was three years younger than I, and my brother Jerry, who was eight years younger. We often had pillow fights and would also wrestle, making noise. When my mother or father would yell up and ask, "What's going on up there?" Grandpa Lazarus would cover for us, saying, "I'm just showing them a few tricks!"

Grandpa Lazarus was a quiet man who no longer worked but always managed to give us his spare change for candy. We enjoyed having Grandpa around, but I recall hearing my mother at one point telling my father that she felt she never had any privacy.

We had been living in even tighter circumstances earlier, when my father's sister, Aunt Myn, also lived with us, but lo and behold, Aunt Myn ended up marrying my mother's brother. (That's right; my mother's brother married my father's sister!) Aunt Myn moved out. Uncle Jack and Aunt Myn were not able to have children, and growing up, it was as though we had two sets of parents.

Uncle Jack and his brother, Uncle Stanley owned one of the largest toy stores in north Jersey—Silver's Save-mor Toyland on Central Avenue in Jersey City. Central Avenue was a long, bustling business street in the city, and there were many retail stores. The toy store itself was large and encompassed three floors: two for toys and one for juvenile furniture and carriages during the Christmas season. All of us— my mom, dad, and brothers—worked there every Christmas season from the beginning of November through Christmas Eve. Mom worked full time, and everyone else in the family worked part time, seven days a week. I recall starting when I was too young to have working papers and my "pay" was my first 35mm camera; my choice, an Argus A-4.

Like every family, we had traditions. Every night when Dad came home from work, one of us would ride our bike down to Mittleman's Bakery to get a fresh rye bread for dinner. We would eat; Dad would go into the den, read the paper and watch television; and after we did our homework, we would go back downstairs to join our parents in the den.

The Barcalounger in the den, designated by my father as *his* chair, was *our* income source. My brothers and I never tried sitting in it when he was around, but when he wasn't around, we'd scoop up all of the change that had fallen out of his pockets and into the base of the chair. We would collect the money every night, and then at the end of the week, we'd split it up between us. It was usually quite a haul!

My best friend early on and throughout my teens was our skinny neighbor, Jimmy Brokey. He and I learned to ride two-wheel bicycles together. Jimmy's family had more money than mine, and he was the only friend I had whose parents could afford to send him away to summer camp. I remember the humongous trunk he had lying in front of his bed. His mother used to pack all his clothes in it for his summer away.

My brothers and I, along with most of my friends, stayed home summers and played at the local playgrounds. We were one of the lucky families who could afford to go to Bradley Beach on the Jersey Shore staying in a rooming house for the month of August. We had our own private bedrooms and shared the bathrooms, showers, and dining room. Each family had its own refrigerator. The rooming house bustled with new people coming and going, and I made some lifelong friends. My dad would come on Friday nights and drive back home to Hillside on Sunday nights or Monday mornings to return to work.

Bradley Beach had a boardwalk, great wide beaches, penny arcades, and a pavilion; dances were held on Friday nights, which attracted all of the teenagers. That was a very big deal for us. So was earning money. We collected bottles on the beach for the two-cent bottle refunds. When I was old enough, fourteen, I became a junior lifeguard there. One year, the crotchety old landlady who owned all the houses in the area rented my Uncle Jack and Aunt Myn a house for the entire summer. We were lucky enough to stay with them for that entire summer that year.

***

As we grew older, Jimmy and I became friends with tall and lanky Harold Rosensweig. The three of us became inseparable. We did everything together, including starting a business to do odd jobs and mow lawns. We even had business cards printed with the saying, "Any Job, Big or Small, We do It Right or Not At All." We mowed lawns and did gardening, cleaned attics and basements. The earnings were important for us, as we were all fifteen years old and needed a source of income. One of our teachers, the head of the music department, hired us to dig up his front and backyard so it could be reseeded and rolled. We gave him a fixed price. We did not realize how difficult a job it was. All three of us wound up with blisters on both hands. We wanted to quit without finishing the job, but our reputation would be shot—in the community and in school as well, since he was a teacher. We had oozing sores for weeks.

Before we were able to drive, we took a bus trip to Washington, DC. Poor Harold got stuck holding some woman's baby for the entire four-hour-plus trip. When we arrived at our motel, we took a nap, waking at dusk thinking, for some reason, it was dawn and we had slept through the night and missed dinner. We asked someone where we could get breakfast, only to discover it was 7:40 p.m., not a.m.!

Hillside, New Jersey was a relatively small town with a population of approximately 26,000, a place where shopkeepers knew their clientele and vice versa. From the time I was little, I often went with my father to pick something up at the drugstore. We were always greeted warmly by the pharmacist, Lenny Auerbach, in his crisp white coat. He knew exactly what we needed, taking the time to talk to us, asking about our family and our health. When he filled our prescriptions, he wrapped them in wrapping paper, the old-fashioned way. He would take a piece of wrapping paper, place it on the counter and take the items and wrap them like a gift package with tape. He would never think of using a bag for those medications he dispensed. I think remembering his demeanor is what prompted me to choose pharmacy as my chosen field of study. He was a charming man, and his knowledge of medicines impressed me. From an early age, I wanted to be a pharmacist.

After graduating from high school, I went to Rutgers University in New Brunswick, New Jersey, with that goal in mind. However, after my freshman year, I discovered that to continue with pharmacy as a major, I needed to transfer to Rutgers University's College of Pharmacy in Newark. It would be like applying to a whole new college. On the other hand, the New England College of Pharmacy (NECP) in Boston, Massachusetts, had a *trimester* program, where you could do three semesters in one year. That seemed perfect. There was one big glitch—I had to be accepted. Another problem was that the pharmacy major had been changed all over the country from a four-year major to a five-year major.

And then there was the regional culture shock. I drove to Boston with my mother for my interview at NECP. It was a very warm day, and we stopped for a cold drink at Manet Lake Pharmacy, a drugstore across from Boston College. At the fountain, I asked for a cherry soda and was served a cherry ice-cream soda. This was my introduction to Boston's interpretation of *soda*, which was totally different from the New Jersey/New York version. In New Jersey, a cherry soda was just cherry syrup and seltzer. Boy, was I in for a surprise when I arrived in New England to learn the difference between a frappe, a milkshake, and a malted milk.

As good fortune had it, I was accepted to NECP, moved to Boston, and became comfortable with their sodas and colloquialisms.

I did not have an easy schedule. While going to school I worked thirty to sixty hours a week at a pharmacy in order to pay my way through college. But I liked the work, and I managed to have time for a social life too. At school I joined a fraternity, Rho Pi Phi, and I became friendly with several guys from Chelsea, Massachusetts. Out with them one day at Fisherman's Beach in Swampscott, I was introduced to a vivacious and very pretty and very petite—four foot ten—blue-eyed girl named Nancy Walk. She not only had a great personality, she was a terrific dancer. I loved to dance. I was smitten. My fraternity brother Mike Greenspoon, from Bridgeport, Connecticut, was equally smitten with Nancy's friend, Judy Rocke. When I told him I'd decided to ask Nancy to the Rho Pi Phi social the following week, Mike said, "I'll ask Judy." He did, and we went together.

I called Nancy during the week, and we talked on the phone for a very long time. She told me she had gone to the University of Miami for her freshman year, didn't like it, and was now back home, deciding where she wanted to go next.

Our personalities seemed to fit, but our backgrounds were not similar. I came from very humble surroundings. I'd worked for everything I had. I'd taken out student loans for my college tuition that I would have to pay off upon graduation. On the other hand, Nancy lived in a big house, had her own new white Plymouth convertible and a family who paid for everything. Those differences didn't seem to matter much. We saw more and more of each other, having great times bowling—either alone or with her friends—double-dating with married couples she knew—Audrey and Steven Scheck, Glen and Peter Brownstein— going to the movies, and dancing at the Bay Tower Room at the top of 60 State Street in Boston. We would often go out for dinner at Jack and Marion's, a delicatessen where young adults hung out on weekend nights, a place to be seen.

On New Year's Eve December, 1961, Mike Greenspoon and I had invited Nancy and her friend Judy Rocke to New

Jersey to celebrate with us. My parents got to meet Nancy. They thought she was adorable. "If you're happy, I'm happy," my mother told me.

And I was happy. I was in love for the first time in my life. Lying together on the couch in her parents' house one night I told her so. Although it is normally most proper to ask the parents of the bride for permission to marry their daughter first, I did it in reverse. "I'm really in love with you," I said, "and I would like to spend the rest of my life with you. Will you marry me?"

I think she was totally surprised. She said yes. I had not been at all nervous when I asked, but I did get a little nervous when she accepted my proposal. This was a big step, and we were very young—twenty years old. But it was what I wanted. When her parents came home that night, I told them that I had asked Nancy to marry me and then I asked their permission.

They were sweet and enthusiastic. They told me they were happy to give their permission. They felt their daughter had made a very good choice. It was a warm moment.

For the engagement, I bought Nancy a cocktail ring, (a less-expensive-than-a-diamond ring.) It was all I could afford. The warmth grew colder for a while. Her mother thought she should have a fancier ring.

Nancy's mother, Adeline Walk, was a tiny woman—also only about four foot ten inches tall—with very blond hair, clothes that were chosen to make a statement, and a personality many times larger than her size. She could turn on the sweetness at will, and she could turn it off even faster. Social-standing was extremely important to her, and while she saw promise in me, she was not pleased with my humble origins.

By contrast, Nancy's father, Arthur, was a quiet, soft-spoken gentleman who rarely made waves. He was also, like his wife, short of stature but very muscular. He'd had cancer about five years before I met Nancy—metastatic melanoma, resulting in a large scar on his neck. At the time the doctors had given him only a short time to live, but he ended up actually outliving three of the doctors who had operated on him.

Nancy and I were married on May 19, 1963, just before my senior year. The wedding was a big extravaganza, planned completely by Adeline. The guest list was tightly controlled to include many more guests from the bride's side than the groom's. My parents were good about that, but they really wanted to walk me down the aisle. Their feelings were hurt when it was nixed by Adeline. I went along with my mother-in-law's orders, because I knew Nancy was extremely close to her mother and I was in love with Nancy. We went to the Neville Country Club in the Catskills for our honeymoon. It was what I could afford.

Nancy's older brother, Randy, who had been a fraternity brother of mine at NECP, had already graduated. In my senior year, he asked if I wanted to become partners with him to buy a pharmacy. Naturally, I said yes, but I did not have any money. He said his parents would lend us the money to buy a store.

We went looking for stores and found a large one we really liked, but the Walks could not understand you didn't need to pay all cash for a store. It was all right to have a note for the balance, if the store was doing a large volume of business. They insisted we get something smaller. We relented and bought Sutherland Pharmacy in Brighton, a section of Boston, and we changed the name to Sutherland Apothecary.

The store was a relatively small one, but as you entered, to the right was a low soda fountain with about eight seats and to the left, a payphone, which was always occupied by salesmen making appointments to sell aluminum siding. The pharmacy department, where the prescriptions were filled, was in the rear of the store. We remodeled and removed the soda fountain, even though, in the Greater Boston area, it was a very common fixture in the 1950s and 1960s.

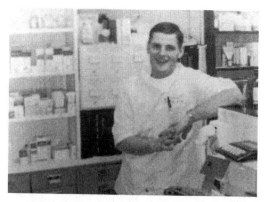

Sutherland Apothecary 1964

I was so excited about the new venture that I made the mistake of inviting my favorite uncle, Jack, to see the pharmacy. After all, the man who had been named New Jersey Toy Retailer of the Year would obviously have some advice to offer his nephew about marketing the store. *Obviously* turned out to be an understatement.

Randy and I showed him around the store and the neighborhood when he arrived. Uncle Jack roared in like a bull in a china closet. "Too small," he said, shaking his head and looking around. "Bigger is better, guys."

"But, Uncle Jack, we're just starting—

"What's behind that wall over there?"

"Another store."

"My suggestion is to take over that store, knock down the wall, and expand."

"But we have no—"

"Gotta *expand*, Harvey," he broke in, making a face, looking around with a frown. "Not gonna be successful with a store this size."

I looked at Randy.

He looked away.

Jack walked around shaking his head. "What's this doing here?" he asked, pointing to one counter. "Gotta remodel too."

"We've already made plans—"

"Hey! Do I know how to sell product? Does the number-one retailer know how to market?"

"Well, marketing is different from remodeling," I pointed out.

"Okay, you want my marketing advice? You *know* my marketing rule! Never give away your product, or if you do, don't be cheap, be ridiculously cheap. Remember that time I advertised one-pound cans of coffee for forty-nine cents a can? I had people lined up around the block to get into my store. That's how you create traffic!"

We just stared at him.

"What's the normal retail price for Maalox?" he asked.

"Three dollars, but CVS sells it for $1.49."

He leaned closer to me. "Run an ad that you're selling it for 79 cents."

"Are you crazy?" I yelled "We will lose $1.21 per bottle!"

"So what?" He grinned. "If you are lucky enough to sell 2,000 bottles, your loss will be only $2,420!"

He wouldn't stop. On and on he went with suggestions that felt a lot like demands. I tried to tell him it was our store. We had to learn certain things by ourselves. We had just taken over only two weeks before, and he had to give us a chance to breathe, but he would not listen. He was adamant about his plans and ideas. And he would not stop. My head was spinning. In the end, I had only one recourse. After listening to his suggestions, I threw him out of the store.

I did not speak again to my beloved uncle Jack for many, many months. Finally, I drove to New Jersey to see him. I apologized for throwing him out of the store, but not for *why* I did it. "Uncle Jack, I know you wanted to protect me, but there are times in one's life that a person has to learn from his or her own mistakes; it is part of growing up."

I was partners with Randy for three years: one year while I was still a senior in pharmacy school and two years after I graduated, a licensed pharmacist. I truly enjoyed the experience. I always enjoyed filling prescriptions, both the science part of knowing about the medications, dosages, and drug interactions, and also the human part of knowing a patient's history with other medicines to make sure there was nothing that would cause a problem. I especially loved the interaction with the customers. Like the neighborhood pharmacist of my childhood, I developed very close personal relationships with most of the families who were regulars in our pharmacy.

Balancing work and study was difficult. I spent many a nights staying up until two or three o'clock in the morning, studying, then going to my classes, and then at two or three in the afternoon going to our store in Brighton. It was about a fifteen-minute drive. I worked until nine p.m. before driving the thirty minutes home to Chelsea. During my senior year, I worked as a pharmacy *technician* and could fill prescriptions as long as a licensed pharmacist was there working the same hours. Randy was easy going and very personable. He was also very technologically savvy.

Trying to build up the business, Randy and I came up with the idea of advertising generic drugs (the cheaper, non-brand-name equivalent for many brand-name drugs). The use of generic drugs was just beginning in the Greater Boston area. We took out a small, one-column-inch ad in the *Boston Globe*. All it said was "Generic Drugs?" and the name, address, and phone number of our store.

Before placing the advertisement, we had gone to New York to visit one of the largest manufacturers of generic drugs in the country. Since generic drugs were relatively new on the horizon, we were concerned about liability and choosing the correct vendor. We made sure they had proper liability insurance. We also made sure that we had additional liability insurance. Once we did our research, we stocked our pharmacy with an extensive inventory of generic drugs.

About a week or so after this small, one-inch ad appeared in the *Globe*, we got a visit from an inspector of the State Board of Pharmacy. He said, "If you do not remove that ad, I'll find enough violations in the store to close you for a year."

At that time, the Board of Pharmacy's position regarding advertising was you could not imply that one pharmacy looked better than another. You could not intimate that only you had generic drugs and others did not. Such a position was not necessarily correct, but since this was their position, they wanted the ad removed.

Given lack of financial resources it would take to fight this injustice legally, we removed the ad.

Approximately six to nine months later, the chain store CVS took the Board of Pharmacy to court about advertising generic drugs, and as they say, the rest is history. In the end the store was sold to a college fraternity brother of ours. From that tiny little one-time advertisement in the *Globe*, some fifteen years later he was still refilling generic drug prescriptions for those longtime customers.

In addition to working in the pharmacy and going to school during my senior year, I was also married and living with my in-laws. Moving in with them allowed us to save money from not having to pay for rent or food.

Soon after we were married, Nancy went for a gynecological exam. The doctor told her she had something wrong with her fallopian tubes. She would not be able to have children. This was absolutely devastating news to both of us. I suggested she make an appointment to see a specialist in Boston. Adeline took over, looking for the right one, but before anything could be done to remedy the problem, Nancy miraculously became pregnant. I was overjoyed ... and also a little frightened by the sudden sense of responsibility—actually more than a little frightened, a lot frightened.

Preparing for life as a future father, I purchased my first life insurance policy. Next door to where I was working was an independent insurance agent, Max Lefkowith. Max gave me a book to read on life insurance, and then he sold me a $100,000 whole-life policy. I paid it in monthly installments. Though payments were relatively low, for me they felt like a fortune. However, I knew I needed to do it to protect my now-growing family. This was my first foray into the world of life insurance, but it would not be my last.

Nancy's mother had an opinion about everything. This included the furniture we should buy for the coming baby. Uncle Jack, who was in the juvenile furniture business, kindly offered to give us a carriage and a crib as gifts. He wanted to send us the best quality and brand available in the market place. He suggested the crib be white so we could use it in the future with any color scheme, no matter what sex this child or future children might be.

"No," Adeline insisted. "I think it should be blue, because I'm certain you're going to have a boy."

"Mom!" I shouted in exasperation. "We shouldn't look a gift horse in the mouth. After all, this is something he is *giving* us. He's been in the juvenile furniture business for over thirty years and knows more about baby furniture than you!"

"You shouldn't talk to my mother that way!" Nancy said, bursting into tears.

There were moments, living with my in-laws that brought back memories of hearing my mother tell my father that she felt that she never had any privacy.

There were also some amusing aspects of living there. Nancy had an elderly great aunt, Aunt Riv, who stopped by every Friday afternoon around four p.m., dressed in her drab long dress and oversized gray coat. She always stopped to drop off some traditional Jewish food (*gribbeness* fried chicken skin and onions) and have a little drink of *schnapps*. I was never sure if it was to drop off the food or to have the drink. Her definition of a "little drink" was about eight ounces of straight scotch with no ice or water. She would come in, drop off her goodies, and then she would down the entire glassful in one whole swallow, after which she would give everyone a kiss, turn to us, and say, "*Kinder* [children], I will see you next week!" and then leave.

On March 15, 1964, our son, Jessie, was born. We were delighted, but even in joy there was a little controversy. Nancy's mother did not want to have a *bris*, which is a traditional Jewish circumcision ceremony for a newborn son. However, I insisted on it. We had the bris at the hospital. Jessie's pediatrician, a family friend of Adeline and Arthur, the grandparents, performed it, and our parents, brothers, and a few very close friends attended.

Nancy experienced migraine headaches postpartum and was in and out of the hospital at least five times, seeing specialists and neurologists. I was studying for my pharmacology final exam. As a result of what I'd learned, I suggested to the neurologist at Mass General Hospital she try giving her Fiorinal. Amazingly, it worked, and it worked for years thereafter. It proved to be an effective therapy for her headaches.

Because of the severity of Nancy's migraines, Mary Windsor, the nurse we hired when Jess was born, stayed with us for about three months to take care of both mother and child. Nancy was in and out of the hospital several times before the headaches went away. Mary was a very wise old woman who had taken care of more babies than Adeline could count. Whenever Adeline gave her advice on taking care of little Jess, Mary would give me a little wink and roll her eyes, knowing I knew what she was thinking. Mary would let Adeline go on and then just do what she wanted to do. "Harvey," she'd tell me time and again, "just let her talk; then walk away."

When I graduated, we found an apartment in Chelsea, near Nancy's parents. Once we moved out, things did get a bit more private … although the Walks had a habit of stopping by unannounced to show off their new grandson to friends. This habit of unannounced stopping by continued unabated as long as Adeline was alive.

***

As Uncle Jack had loudly pointed out, our pharmacy was a small one, and I was now married, with a baby and another one on the way, and earning fifty dollars a week. I needed to supplement my income. Nancy's father had made all his money in the "remainder book business." When publishers had printed too many magazines or paperback books and sent them to their distributors, they were sold on a guaranteed basis. If they did not sell, the distributor would tear off the front cover (or part of the front cover) and return the cover for credit. The distributor would then discard the remaining part of the magazines and books to wastepaper companies. These wastepaper companies were supposed to destroy the leftovers—some even were made to sign contracts promising to destroy them—but most had no such contracts and opted to sell the remnants instead.

That's where my father-in-law came in. He bought up publishers' overstocked magazines, paperback books, and comic books from the wastepaper companies in bulk, and resold them individually. My father-in law was not ready to retire, but I saw how lucrative the book business could become and thought this could readily be expanded. There was enough business out there for me to earn a lot of money without cutting into his livelihood.

He agreed, so long as I developed my own customers. "I will take you out for one morning and show you what I do," he told me. "But after that, you are on your own."

We agreed I would take out the back seat of my car, fill my car with inventory from his warehouse—magazines, comics, and books to sell during my off hours from the store. I would pay him at the end of the week—on Friday—from my profits for the amount of goods I'd taken.

In his sixties, Arthur was still strong enough to throw around piles of books as though they were feathers. "As I've told you before, the publishers will threaten you. They'll say 'we are going to put you out of business.'" he said. "But I've been doing this for almost fifty years and nothing has happened. Furthermore, my attorneys have assured me there is absolutely nothing illegal in what I'm doing. They have researched all of the necessary statutes."

It was understandable publishers felt the way they did. The major publishers of paperback books were impacted dramatically. For example, the full retail price of a book was $5.95 when sold in stores, while my father-in-law sold the same books for 49 cents—without a front cover but with the full spine of the book and of course all the text. Quite a price differential!

"Dad," I said as I looked at his piles of inventory, "it's crazy for you to be doing all this by hand. Shouldn't we buy a forklift?"

"Don't be silly," he scoffed. "The place is too small for a forklift."

He had no qualms about my working in the business with him, but he was very resistant to change.

"This is fabulous!" he said later, when I convinced him to get a forklift. "I don't know why we didn't get one sooner."

Just months after I entered the remainder book business, I was getting more calls to reorder books than I was getting to fill prescriptions. It turned out I loved business more than I loved filling prescriptions (pharmacy/pharmacology). Perhaps, if our store had been a thriving high-volume store, my attitude would have been different. I told my wife I wanted to try selling books fulltime and work part time as pharmacist. Reluctantly, she agreed. My parents were not happy that I was giving up pharmacy to go into the book business. However, I explained to them that I would maintain my pharmacy license and could always work as a pharmacist if things did not work out. I valued my education in pharmacy.

Moving on into the book business full time, I gave my interest in the drugstore to my brother-in-law, Randy. Randy then sold the store to pursue a career path he had always wanted, entering dental school at the age of thirty. He ultimately becoming a successful dentist.

I loved being in the book business. I got up every morning at five a.m. and got to the warehouse to make sure the trucks were loaded for the day's routes. My father-in-law had been a one-man show, but as my customers multiplied, I had to hire additional help to handle all of them. The customers had to be seen every two weeks. I also developed business with chain stores, which required large deliveries. Therefore, I needed additional vehicles to service those accounts. I also began servicing people in the industry in other parts of the country. I was very careful. I only purchased from companies that had *not* signed contracts promising to destroy the leftovers. Therefore, we're not violating any laws.

I also bought excess production for cash directly from publishers who had overruns and just wanted to get rid of the excess for wastepaper with no restrictions. They would never disclose to their regular distributors they were doing so, because this would have had the distributors in an uproar. Many of the deals I made were with high-level executives.

My customers were primarily small variety stores, candy stores, convenience stores, liquor stores, five-and-ten-cent stores, discount stores, and health-and-beauty-aid stores, but I also did business with mass-market chain stores as well.

While I loved making the sales and boosting my earnings, I realized the book business was not providing me with enough intellectual challenge. In 1967, I decided I wanted to go to graduate school to obtain a master's degree in business administration ... but get it slowly. Our daughter, Lauryn, was born just a few months after I made my decision. With my business and growing family I could not go to school full time, or anything resembling full time.

The first place I applied to was my alma mater, Northeastern University. I went in for an interview and was told by the admissions officer I would have no problem being admitted since I had been a dean's list student my last two years of their pharmacy school.

I also applied to and was accepted by two other graduate MBA programs, but it turned out they were thesis programs. Since during my entire undergraduate career I had to write only three papers and suffered through the writing of them, I had absolutely no interest in a thesis program.

By early August, I had not heard from Northeastern, and I called the admissions officer whom I'd met earlier. "Didn't you get our letter stating we wanted you to first take two or three liberal arts courses before we would consider you for admission?" he asked

"No, I did not." I said. "And you have to be kidding."

I then went to Suffolk University to meet with the dean of the Graduate School of Business Administration. After his review of my records and our interview, he asked me why Suffolk. I told him the truth: no thesis, convenience. I also told him I was going to take one course at a time per semester. He told me I would be accepted. The dean had warned me that those students who took the program part time, one course per semester, had less than a 5 percent chance of completing the program through graduation. Needless to say, I am very proud to have proved him wrong. I obtained my MBA from Suffolk University on June 10, 1972.

***

I was paying for the education myself, unlike most of the others in my class, who had to worry about maintaining a B average so that their companies would reimburse them for their tuition. However, I had decided that I just wanted to sit back and soak up all the information the courses had to offer, without the pressure of having to worry about the grades. I did whatever assignments were required but did not do all of the necessary readings. I did attend all of the classes and took all the exams.

I recall in one class in particular, one of the professors, a former executive with Dunkin Donuts, told the class many franchisees cheat on their franchisors. He said they did not report all of their sales and put some of their cash sales into their pockets. The people in the class, all of whom worked for large corporations, were aghast. He looked at me and said, "Lazarus, since you are the only one in the class who is an entrepreneur with real-life experience, tell them what it is like in the real world!"

***

After working in the remainder book business for approximately five years, I offered to buy out Nancy's father's interest. He was ready to retire, but Nancy's mother refused to allow him to put the stock in my name.

"Mom," I said finally, after the discussion had been going on long enough. I wanted to explain how putting a value on the business now while Arthur was alive would confer a more realistic value than if a disinterested party (like the IRS) came to put a value on the business after his death. "If something were to happen to Arthur and the IRS came and put a value on the stock based on your lifestyle, your daughter would have to come up with $200,000 or $300,000 in taxes to transfer the stock. Is that what you want?"

She finally saw the light, I purchased the business by paying Arthur an annual lifetime pension of a proportion of his annual salary. This pension would be paid for out of the profits of the business. The business was a cash cow.

We had been operating out of a small 2,500 square-foot building in Chelsea, Massachusetts. I then purchased an 18,000 square-foot building located in Salem that had been an old auto dealership. Unknowingly, this was my entry into the real-estate-development business. Nancy's father thought it was crazy for me to want to buy such a large building, to move my business there, and incur a mortgage and overhead to expand the business, but I thought he'd once again probably change his mind once he saw it working.

The year 1971 began very auspiciously. Our third child, Gregg, was born on January 25—to the delight of us and his two older siblings—and his four-year-old sister, Lauryn, got a name change. Nancy was shopping one day at Jordan Marsh in the North Shore Mall, with Gregg in his stroller and Lauryn tagging along. Our little girl had ringlets in her hair, and one of the sales girls said, "Oh my God, she looks just like Buffy from the TV program *Family Affair*!"

Other sales people began gathering around, saying, "You are right!"

From that point on, Lauryn was Buffy.

As the year continued, it took a turn for the worse. Lo and behold, six years after I had gone into the business fulltime, I was sued for "illegally reselling publications and copyright infringement" by two publishers, Gulf Western and the Hearst Corporation. A sheriff showed up on my doorstep to deliver the summons and complaints. I opened the envelopes, read the enclosed charges, which were several pages long, and sat down. I wasn't sure what to think about it or even what to do first.

I called Nancy. "You are not going to believe this," I told her, "but I just got sued by two Fortune 100 publishers."

She gasped. "What are you going to do?"

"I am going to look for a lawyer to represent me. I am also going to stop by your father's house and see what he thinks."

Arthur Walk waved the summons away with a toss of his hand. "Oh, they have been threatening for fifty years," he said. "It is probably a bluff."

"This is not a bluff … this is for real! What if I end up being put out of business or, even worse, in jail?"

"I told you, you're not doing anything illegal." He shook his head. "Trust me; nothing will come of it. Relax."

"Relax?! Easy for you to say. When did you ever get served with a summons like this?"

He nodded, slowly understanding. "Never," he admitted meekly.

However, the publishers' lawsuit was one of those nightmares with a life of its own. The wheels of litigation spin very slowly and little happened for a long time, but it was always there, looming large, hanging over my head.

I took Nancy and Jess with me to the first major deposition at the law offices of Bingham, Dana & Gould in Boston. I wanted them to understand the kind of stress and pressure I was feeling, and I thought firsthand observation would help demonstrate that.

The strategy worked—by the end of the day's proceedings they certainly understood. But it was an exasperating day. I underwent nonstop questioning from four different lawyers from three different Park Avenue law firms. My attorney, Joe Kay, kept objecting to certain questions, and at one point, to the entire line of questioning.

When they asked about a particular supplier of mine from New Bedford, they pronounced and then spelled out his name. I asked them to repeat the spelling. My attorney kicked me under the table. They had pronounced the name incorrectly and spelled it completely wrong. Therefore, I could truthfully answer I did not do business with anyone by that name from New Bedford. That was the one high point for me. The rest was intense pressure, answering question after question posed by a large group of intimidating attorneys.

Adding to the tension the lawsuit created for my family and me, Nancy's mother, Adeline, was diagnosed with mycosis fungoides, also known as Alibert-Bazin syndrome or granuloma fungoides, the most common form of cutaneous T-cell lymphoma. Mycosis fungoides generally affects the skin, but may progress internally to the organs over time. Symptoms included rashes, tumors, skin lesions, and itchy skin.

Neither Nancy nor I realized the disease was fatal until we looked it up. When we did, we found out it was eventually a fatal disease, though the lifespan of one afflicted with this disease could be quite long. Although there was no cure, there were treatments that could mitigate the itching to the point where it was bearable, perhaps even prevent the disease from progressing. At the time, the only known treatment was specialized ultraviolet phototherapy. Nancy, therefore, began taking her mother for radiation and the ultraviolet photo treatments once or twice every week. Nancy also made several turbans with bangs for Adeline to wear so nobody could tell she had lost her hair.

Other than that, my family life was a pleasant distraction from the lawsuit. Jess and Buffy were very protective of their little brother. It was so sweet to observe them with Gregg. Buffy and her best friend, Judi Brown (who lived across the street from us), loved to take Gregg for walks in the stroller around the neighborhood and babysit for him.

When he was seven, Jess had begun playing the drums. After driving him to private drum lessons with one of the best teachers in the area every Tuesday evening for years, I decided I was going to join him and take a lesson right after his. As a child, I had taken drum lessons but never got beyond a drum pad, partly because my parents could not afford to buy a set of drums. However, my desire to take lessons from my son's teacher was not just to do what I'd always wanted to do, but rather to get good enough to be able to play a duet with Jess at his Bar Mitzvah party. We ended up accomplishing this and to rave reviews! What a thrill for both of us!

That, however, was the way the kids were in the *early* years of the lawsuit. Finally, in the end, *nine years* after the original summons, just as we were supposed to go to trial, the publishers dropped the charges. Nothing underscores the passage of time quite as dramatically as children. The kids grew quickly and dramatically during the course of the lawsuit, and Gregg went from being an adorable infant to a nine-year-old with a personality all on his own. Adorable little Buffy had matured into a vivacious teenager, avid tennis player, and studious student. Jess was captain of the Swampscott High School Golf Team, co-captain of the tennis team, and starting to decide where to apply for college.

Jess was also a teenager—a teen with good and bad connotations, mostly good in Jess's case, but teenagers are teenagers. When he was nineteen years old, he got caught sitting in his old, dark-blue Volvo with an "illegal drug" (as they called it in those days), with three of his friends. They had been at a party across the street at the home of one of those friends, whose father happened to be a cop in Marblehead. The police took them into custody at the Marblehead police station. I was called, along with the other boy's father, the police officer. We went down to the station. We arranged for the clerk magistrate to set a court appearance for them in two weeks. We were lucky to get the charges dropped, but Jess didn't know that. I told Jess we needed to get a criminal attorney. I said I'd lay out the money for the attorney's fee but Jess would have to sign a note and eventually pay me back. I hired Boston criminal defense attorney David Miltz and called him ahead of time, telling him the charges had been dropped but that I wanted him to scare the shit out of the kids.

He gave a solid performance, explaining they might not be able to go to college and could get charged with possession of drugs, a felony. His fee to appear at the court was five hundred dollars. However, at my request, he gave me a bill for five thousand dollars and then sent me a bill in the mail with a $4,500 courtesy discount. I made Jess sign a note for the $5,000 and kept it in my safe deposit box until his twenty-first birthday, when I told him the truth and the whole story.

Nine years was an extraordinarily long time to feel under the gun of a lawsuit. In the end, if I won by having them back down, the publishers had, nonetheless, accomplished their goal. They had made me decide to think about closing my book business and start a new chapter of my life.

Chapter 2

HOW I BECAME A
REAL-ESTATE DEVELOPER

"I've found a great little business I'm thinking of buying," I told my wife one evening. "It's the world's largest producer of ear muffs."

Nancy blinked. "Come again? Ear muffs?"

I explained it was very profitable, and furthermore, ear muffs had just come back into style. They were no longer the old-fashioned variety that came with curled up steel bands always catching in your hair. No, the latest version came in bright-colored fabrics, some even made of fancy materials such as expensive mink fur and carried by high-end department stores at exorbitant prices.

The producer of ear muffs whose business I was considering buying did not manufacture any of the components. He only assembled pieces that he had manufactured by outside vendors, employing immigrant workers from Russia in a facility on Lincoln Street in downtown Boston.

I had all the financing arranged ... and then I got cold feet.

"Self," I said, "this is the fashion business, of which you know nothing, and you are about to sign for a loan in excess of two hundred thousand dollars; if you fail, you will never come back from a loss this big. Are you out of your mind?"

The short answer to that question was ... no. I bid ear muffs adieu, no matter how attractive they'd become over the years. But I needed something—preferably something I knew more about than manufacturing ear muffs. I looked at my wife and children and worried about the future.

Then I realized I had managed to purchase and profit from a successful piece of real estate for my book business. I decided I had some experience in real estate, with success.

If I found more property and developed it—if it went well—I could make a bundle. If it did not go well, I might lose some money. But even if had to sign personally for a loan of two hundred thousand plus, I would probably not lose all of it. Why not look around?

I assumed it would take me six to eight months to find a property that would be to my liking. Happily (lo and behold), I found what I thought was a great property only two weeks later. It was the old Pepsi-Cola bottling plant, known as the Elk Springs Bottling Company, in Wakefield, Massachusetts.

The building was on a nonconforming parcel of land with an old warehouse. A "nonconforming parcel of land" means it did not fit the existing zoning regulations: it was an anomaly. The building itself was my kind of building—an old warehouse nobody wanted. I envisioned subdividing it for smaller tenants and putting a new skin on it to make it look like a modern building. This was an area in which I had some expertise. The real-estate market in the area was strong for owner-occupied office space. I figured the piece of land on the corner of this parcel would lend itself to a 15,000 square-foot office-condominium building. Since just for the price of the building I would be getting all of the land as well, we were basically getting the land for free. We would still be making a net cash-flow profit on the building.

I borrowed five thousand dollars on a credit card and signed a purchase-and-sale agreement subject to a forty-five-day financing clause. This would allow me to get out of the contract if I could not get financing for the purchase. I had no idea where I was going to go for financing or, truthfully, what my next steps were going to be. I just knew this was a good deal, and I would somehow manage to put it together.

It was a beautiful evening in May when I came home that night. I couldn't wait to tell Nancy about my idea. "You are not going to believe it," I said excitedly, "but I found this fantastic piece of property. I put a deposit on it, and they accepted my offer!"

Her eyes filled with fear. "What do you mean they accepted your offer? What offer?"

I told her the financial details.

"How are you going to pay for it with no money? What makes you think this is such a good property?"

"The property is way undervalued, given the zoning and its location. I know I can make it work. Trust me, if I can put this deal together; we'll be just fine. More than fine!"

"Why not just keep making money in the book business?"

"Because the lawsuit sent us a warning signal the book business might not provide us with a stable income long-term!"

I thought I'd convinced her, but the next night when I got home, her mother was sitting with her in the living room. "Harvey," my mother-in-law said with the conviction of a real-estate expert—and an expert on everything else as well—"you don't know what you're doing. Why buy property? What's wrong with the book business?"

"I'm not giving up the book business," I explained. "I'm looking for a just-in-case scenario: just in case the book business stops being such a stable source of income. I still have a lot of work to do before I get the property. I have to get financing and create a business plan and an architectural plan—"

"What are you, crazy? Buying a parcel of land that cost almost a million dollars?"

"Well, at the moment, I've only put down a five-thousand-dollar deposit."

"Yeah?" Adeline said, her eyes narrowing. "And where exactly did you get the five thousand dollars?"

What I really wanted to say was "it's none of your damn business." Nancy and her mother had long been exerting pressure on me to stay in the book business. Nancy had been depressed lately. I thought perhaps that played a role in her hesitancy, but as we argued, I realized her mother, and the power she exerted over her daughter, was behind it. The argument went on and on. It concluded by her mother insisting I was completely out of my mind and I needed to set up an appointment with the psychologist in Salem who had been treating Nancy for her depression. (Adeline had also gone to see him a few times to deal with her disease.)

I scheduled an appointment. At the end of the session, the psychologist pronounced me stable—no apparent mental disorders. He said that my wife, however, needed help. There were serious control issues regarding her mother. It might be helpful, he said, to assert myself more in the marriage and keep Adeline out of it. He recommended that Nancy see a psychiatrist who could prescribe medication for her depression. He also recommended we go together to a marriage counselor, which we did.

I considered my "being mentally healthy" diagnosis a signal to go ahead with the real-estate deal. I put together some plans, projections, and pro-forma statements, tucked them under my arm, and off I went to five banks with the courage of my convictions.

Much to my chagrin, I was declined by all five.

My next business appointment was with a savings bank in Winchester, number six. This time, I was not surprised when I was once again declined. However, the loan officer suggested that I go upstairs and meet with the president of their development company. He said he thought this was a project that might be of interest to them.

I didn't just walk upstairs; I nearly flew up the stairs. I told the secretary I was referred by the vice president of the bank downstairs. She sent me in, and the president of the development company, Mr. Anthony Pegrucci, saw me right away. "I have seen this piece of junk," he said looking at the papers. "There is nothing you can do with it."

"Oh, yes, there is," I said, and told him about my plans. After explaining my idea, we arrived at a wagered agreement: If I was right, they would provide all the financing and be my partner. If I was wrong, I would buy him and his wife dinner at the restaurant of his choice. I knew I could not lose.

"So what's so special?" he asked at 8:30 the next morning as we stood looking at the property.

"See that corner of the property in front of you?" I said, "You can build a 15,000 square-foot office-condo building on that corner."

He shook his head. "You can't."

"Yes, you can," I countered. "It's a nonconforming parcel." I handed him the zoning regulations and pointed to a clause that allowed measurement to go fifty feet beyond the property boundary for calculations in determining building size.

"You win," he said, after examining everything thoroughly. "What do you want?"

"You provide 100 percent of the financing," I said. "We are 50/50 partners, and I get a developer's fee of sixty thousand dollars."

"Done," he said. "Follow me to the office. We will draft the outline of the agreement for the attorneys to complete."

I wish I could say this first successful real-estate venture was met with joy at home, but both Nancy and her mother acted as though I'd betrayed them. They were extremely upset I had become a man of my own convictions, ignoring their advice. It didn't help that our son Jessie was also asserting himself at that time.

Jess had gone to Hobart College for his freshman year and entered their pre-med program at the forceful suggestion of Nancy and his grandmother, Adeline. Mid-year he was very unhappy. He wanted to quit and change majors. A friend of mine knew the assistant dean of admissions for the Boston University Medical School. Nancy and Adeline thought it would be great if Jess could meet with him. I thought this was a great idea, since I knew the dean would be completely honest with Jess.

When the three of us arrived, he asked Nancy and me to wait outside. He invited our son in to meet with him. Ninety minutes later, Jess came out, and then the dean asked us to come in.

"Jess is extremely smart and capable of doing whatever he wants academically," the dean explained. "I told him to do what he wants to do, not what his mother or grandmother or anyone else wants him to do, if he truly wants to feel fulfilled in life."

Nancy came out of that meeting furious. She was so disappointed, as she thought my friend was going to tell him he should go to Boston University's six-year medical school program to become the doctor that she and his grandmother wanted him to become. Jess wound up transferring to Boston University and majoring in economics; he did just fine.

We were sitting in the living room one night when out of the blue Nancy turned and said to me, "You are not going to believe this. My mother wants to take her own life."

I did a double take. "She wants to do what? How do you know?"

"She asked Randy to help her get the medication she'd need to kill herself. She thought it would be easy for him, because he can write prescriptions."

Randy was Nancy's older brother and my former partner in the pharmacy, now a dentist. "What did Randy say?" I asked.

"He said, 'Absolutely not!' and tried to talk her out of it."

"He could lose his license, as well as his whole practice if he did something like that," I told her. "And what did you say when she told you about her request to Randy?"

"Same thing Randy told her—that she was crazy to think of such a thing. 'If you're feeling that bad,' I told her, 'you need to go to a doctor.'"

"Or a psychiatrist. She's not physically in any pain, is she?"

"No. The itching bothers her, but no pain." Nancy paused for a moment. "She read Betty Rollins's book on how to commit suicide."

"Betty Rollins committed suicide?"

"No. Betty Rollins's mother, Ida, was diagnosed with terminal <u>ovarian cancer.</u> Rollins helped her mother end her life. She wrote about it in her book, *Last Wish*. In her book she provided the recipe of the necessary medications to take one's life. My mother gave me a copy to read so I would know what she was planning to do."

"Did you read it?"

Nancy nodded.

"Nancy, I understand for some people in dire circumstances this assisted suicide is helpful as a last resort, but your mother is not dying of ovarian cancer. She is not in any pain. She's not even dying. She has a chronic condition that provides some discomfort, but even that is being helped by the radiation therapy."

"I know." Nancy sighed.

***

While going through these difficult times at home, I had to struggle with continuing my new business relationships.

The Development Group was a wholly-owned subsidiary of the savings bank in Winchester, and Anthony Pegrucci was president of the Development Group. Almost instantaneously, thanks to having a bank subsidiary as a partner, I became "Joe Developer." We subsequently did three other deals together. We bought two other pieces of land, which I found and resold quickly for substantial profits. The terms for all of the deals I did with Pegrucci were the same; a 50/50 partnership. They put up all of the money and I got a handsome developer's fee.

Our next project was a piece of land I found in Nashua, New Hampshire, on which we created a subdivision known as Fox Run and built twelve single-family homes. At this point, our business had grown rapidly. Tony Pegrucci hired a woman to be his assistant to oversee some of the projects. She and I did not get along. I sensed she was constantly trying to find things wrong with the project. I suspected she wanted to climb the corporate ladder and wanted to get rid of me. I decided to solve the problem myself.

I went to Tony. "Tony, while we are still friends and on good terms, the Wakefield warehouse is not your style of property and building houses is not my style. Why don't we swap properties and end our relationship now, because I fear that your assistant and I are going to end up in a nasty battle."

And so we ended a wonderful relationship on great terms, as all good relationships should end.

I proceeded to do other real-estate deals on my own. I bought a 50,000 square-foot warehouse building in Ward Hill Industrial Park in Haverhill. It had a tenant, Obermeyer Ski Manufacturers, who occupied 75 percent of the building, and a local tenant who occupied the remainder of the building. Both had five-year leases. I was fortunate and obtained 100 percent financing, which was an absolute miracle.

"My mother is going to call you tonight," Nancy told me when I got home from work.

"How come?"

Nancy shrugged. "She just wants to talk to you."

I wondered what I'd done wrong this time. It was about eleven at night when she called. "I just wanted you to know that I love you," she said, "and I want you to keep taking good care of Nancy, the children, and Arthur."

I got off the phone totally perplexed. Was this some form of good-bye? I turned to Nancy. "Is that what I think it is?" I asked.

I got no answer.

I was at the office in Salem, about ten minutes from Swampscott, around noon the next day when Nancy called. "Harvey, do you know where my dad is?"

"He told me he was going to be on the road today, seeing customers."

"Good," she said. "I'm at my parents' condominium. My mother is dead."

45

"What!"

She started crying. "Come quickly."

When I got there, I walked in and found her mother propped up in her bed, gray and cold. I felt for a pulse; there was none. I called 911, and we waited for the police. When they arrived, Nancy told them she had called her mother repeatedly. When there was no answer, she'd become concerned and decided to come over. She'd found her just as she was; then she immediately called me to come over.

Given Nancy's mother's long history dealing with an ultimately fatal disease, it was ruled that Adeline Walk died of natural causes.

That night, I held Nancy as she cried. "I need to tell you something," she said after a while.

"I know," I said, "you miss your mother. That's only normal, given—"

"No. No! That's not it! I helped kill my mother!"

My body chilled. "What do you mean?"

Nancy then told me her mother convinced her to look up the fatal recipe described in the Betty Rollins book. Nancy was to collect the medications by getting prescriptions from various doctors over the course of a year, so that she could help her mother commit suicide when Adeline felt the time was right.

"Why didn't you tell me?" I moaned, holding her in my arms, "I could have helped you get out of doing that. I could have gotten help for both of you!"

Arthur Walk was never told his wife had committed suicide let alone that his daughter had helped her. No one knew except Nancy's brother, Randy. Unlike Nancy, Randy had kept his parents at arm's distance all his life, even as a child. One night, after Adeline died, we went to Randy's house in Arlington, had a long talk with him and his wife, Carol, about his mother. They had been estranged from Adeline for a number of years. Adeline despised Carol and had made no secret of it. She had long been very jealous of Carol's parents, who were wealthy. While Adeline and Arthur were constantly at our house and showered our children with gifts, they rarely saw Carol and Randy's children.

Meeting that night with Carol and Randy, we talked for several hours about Adeline and her personality, how controlling she had been during both Randy's and Nancy's lives as children and through their college years. Nancy and Randy both agreed about that, but the difference was that while Nancy knew her mother was intrusive, she had loved her and now missed her. Nancy cried a lot that night and talked about the guilt she felt for helping her mother take her own life.

The guilt continued to weigh her down. She could not cope with the fact she had helped her mother kill herself. She felt despondent, wasn't eating, had trouble sleeping. She saw both a psychologist and a psychiatrist. Still, Nancy's depression lingered. At one point, the psychiatrist prescribed a combination of drugs that interacted so horribly, we almost had to have

Nancy institutionalized. Fortunately, however, the episode passed.

The turbans Nancy had made for Adeline to cover up her hair loss had been very attractive. For a while, she thought of going into the business of making them pro-bono to help patients losing their hair from chemotherapy and radiation. Her therapists encouraged the idea, hoping it might prove to be a distraction, but as her emotional issues grew and her energy deteriorated, the idea fell by the wayside.

***

Nancy's mental illness began to take up more and more of my time. I decided to bring in a partner to the real-estate business. I thought I could use some help. I had used one real-estate broker, Amos Brantin, exclusively to handle all my transactions. Since Amos had always wanted to get into the real-estate development business, I brought him on. As a team, we became quite successful.

We formed Lazarus, Brantin & Co., Inc. at a time when the Greater Boston real-estate market was booming. I had an affinity for old automobile dealerships. I purchased the old Chelsea Chevrolet dealership on Broadway in Chelsea, converted the building into a multi-tenant building, and leased out all of the space. Then Amos and I developed the old used car lot into twenty-four townhouse condominiums. Those sold out rather quickly as well.

Before we could start construction on that project, we also had to go before the Chelsea Zoning Board of Appeals in the city for a special permit, which we were entitled to and were granted with ease. After completing this project, I was given an award as Man of the Year for Beautification of the City by the Chelsea Chamber of Commerce.

And then, happily, things lightened up at home. Nancy came out of her depression and seemed happy. She began making social engagements with old friends we had not seen for years. She seemed to thrive on our unbelievably busy social schedule, like the old days. She also told me she had spoken with old friends on the telephone, friends she happened to call out of the blue. She also arranged for us to take a family cruise for ten days to the Caribbean. She said since Jess and Buffy were in college, it might be the last time we could all go together on a family vacation. It was very unlike her, vacation planning, but we all had a great time. I recall one night when Gregg was sitting in the lounge of the ship with Jess and Buffy. He put a big cigar in his mouth and ordered a drink, even though he was under age. We had a good laugh!

Nancy also insisted I go and buy the Jaguar I'd always dreamed of owning. Gregg came with me when I picked up the car. We met his mother on the way home, and the three of us went out for dinner together. Nancy looked like her old self— better, even. She looked prettier than she had in years. It was a very happy occasion.

Chapter 3

PERSONAL TRAGEDIES & LOSSES

After a lengthy meeting with our accountants the next day, I returned home and found a note from Nancy, asking me to meet her at my in-laws' apartment. Since my father-in-law was in Florida, it seemed odd to me to meet her at their condominium. The note also said not to bring Gregg—to either let him stay at his friend's house or have him stay at home.

It had been snowing that day. As I drove up the driveway and arrived at the building, I saw her silver-gray Volvo station wagon's windshield was covered with three inches of snow. Suddenly, I got a sick feeling in my stomach and a nightmarish vision of what I was going to find. I ran up the steps.

I opened the door to their apartment and called out her name. "Nancy? Nancy!"

No answer.

I walked into the bedroom, and the nightmare came true. Nancy was lying on the bed in the same room, propped up in exactly the same position her mother had been in when we'd found her. My heart pounded as I ran over.

She wasn't breathing. I felt no pulse. She was cold and blue. I called 911. Then I held her in my arms and sobbed.

Why why why? Gradually, my anguish turned into anger. I wanted to scream, *Look what you've done, Adeline! See what you've done to my wife, my life!* I became so furious I pounded the wall so hard my fist burst through the plaster.

Deciding I needed some help, I dialed 911 again and then I called our close friends, John and Mary Bakis and Peter and Susan Kaker, who rushed over, getting there just after the police and paramedics arrived. The police questioning began: *How did I know to come to the apartment? Had she been despondent? Had she been seeing a psychiatrist? Had she been on medication? Had there been a suicide note?*

"A suicide note?" I hadn't even thought to look. With the police, I looked for a note and found one. It was addressed, "To Harvey Only." In it Nancy said she could not stop feeling guilty for her mother's death, and she was afraid she was becoming more like her mother—too controlling in our lives. She said she loved the four of us very much and felt we would be better off without her.

Why? Why, when she'd been so happy lately? Just last night, she seemed happier and more radiant than I'd seen her in years! Why?

The police told me they would have to hold onto the note for a while, as part of the ordinary course of their investigation. There would have to be an autopsy, which was a routine matter in suicide deaths, but that the autopsy would be done very quickly, probably overnight through blood tests, because a drug overdose was suspected, and since she was Jewish, they knew we would want to be able to have the funeral as soon as possible.

As soon as I got home, I called the kids and told them that something had happened to Mom and that she had died. They had to come home immediately. I told them not to drive by themselves, but either to have a friend drive them or I would send a driver for them. I called Gregg and told him to come home immediately.

When the four of us finally got together, we were all extremely distraught. *Why*, the children wanted to know, *why?* As we sat that night in my bedroom, I tried to explain taking her own life was "an act of love" (even though I couldn't help feeling it was a selfish act). I told them what was in the suicide note (which they eventually got to read after the police released it), namely, Nancy did not want to control their lives the way her mother had controlled hers. She felt it was her only way out, and she felt we would all be better off without her.

That night we all cried together for a very long time. We all would have been better off *with* her, and if we'd only realized, we would have worked together to help her.

Nancy was well known and liked by many in the community. The funeral service was held at Temple Israel in Swampscott, attended by so many people—over 1,200—they had to set up extra chairs, the way they did on the High Holidays.

Buffy was twenty and a sophomore at Boston University. Jess was twenty-three and a senior at BU. Gregg was sixteen and a tenth grader at Swampscott High School. Of the three children, I felt Buffy was the closest to her mother. She was also very close to our family friend, Susan Kaker, and I hoped that Susan would help her through this. I was most worried about Gregg, since he was the youngest and the one who had still been at home with Nancy. He was also the most resistant to getting any type of counseling.

Both Buffy and Jess took a couple of weeks off before returning to school, with the understanding that we would play it by ear. If they wanted to take more time off, they could. They were both good students and missing classes was not an issue. I bought Buffy a car so she could drive home whenever she wanted.

Gregg was very fond of Lilian, the housekeeper we'd had for years. She agreed to work for me full time so she would be at home each day between when Gregg came home from school and I returned from work.

I, my three children, and our entire extended family were stricken with grief. In addition, the entire community was taken aback. Everyone wanted answers. They wanted to blame someone. Some wanted to blame me. Many blamed her therapists for not recognizing she was suicidal. I blamed her mother for continuing to dictate Nancy's actions from the grave.

It is always much easier to blame someone else for a tragedy. In twenty years of practice, the psychologist she was seeing, Dr. Shortin, had never had a patient commit suicide. Nancy was the first. Her suicide took an emotional toll on him too. I saw him for therapy after her death, and he was very helpful. He also helped solve the big question I had been unable to answer: why would a woman who came out of a severe depression, who had been energetic and seemingly happy for six to eight weeks, calling old friends, making social engagements, suddenly kill herself?

It turned out her sudden happiness may have been a sign, but certainly not one we would have recognized. I was told very often those contemplating suicide are at ease with themselves once they have made up their minds they are going to do it, how and where and when. A kind of euphoria sets in. They become at peace within their own body and mind. They almost feel as though they have a halo around them. The radiant happiness she exuded at the restaurant with Gregg and me the previous night might have been because she knew what she was going to do the next day.

As a family, we had to pick up the pieces and move forward with our lives no matter how difficult it was. Jess had to continue with his senior year. Buffy had to finish her sophomore year at Boston University, and Gregg his high school year, all with me not knowing where to begin after being married for twenty-four-plus years. It was a very trying year for us all in so many ways.

I wanted them all to get professional counseling. However Buffy, who was already seeing a counselor, was the only one who embraced the idea. Jess and Gregg resisted but finally relented, though I think with limited success in opening up to the psychologist in dealing with the grieving process. We all had so much to deal with and really didn't know where or how to start.

Though Gregg was always passionate about basketball, he was very short, and both his mother and his grandmother had constantly told him that because of that, he shouldn't build up his hopes. "Think of another sport," they told him. "You're too short to ever make a basketball team."

In September, six months after Nancy's death, Gregg tried out for the basketball team, and he made it. I went to his first game and every game thereafter. In the middle of the first game, I looked up at the ceiling and whispered, "See Nancy? Where there is a will, there is a way; your son did it!"

Back in the business world, Amos and I had put a rather large deposit on a significant piece of land at the corner of Eastern Avenue and Shurtleff Street in Chelsea. We had envisioned a complex of 240 mid-rise, residential condominium units at this location. As a result of the Greater Boston real-estate market boom, it seemed likely the next logical city for gentrification was Chelsea. It was located less than two miles from Boston, less than two miles from Logan Airport, and had easy access to the north, south, and west interstate highway systems.

We hired an architect and engineers, who drew up the preliminary plans. We then found out that we needed, once again, a special permit and would have to go before the Zoning Board of Appeals. Although the attorney we hired from the city of Chelsea told us we had a right to build what we wanted, the special permit was a requirement. The chairman of the Board of Appeals kept delaying our appearance.

One day I got a call from the chairman's office requesting Amos and I meet with him at his place of business. When we arrived, he asked if we could go next door, where it was more private, so we could speak. We began with small talk and pleasantries and then moved on to the project in general.

He talked about how wonderful the project would be for the city. He said he was sorry about all the delays but they had been overwhelmed with other items on the agenda. He finally said he would do what he could do to speed up our application.

"Harvey," he said, as we were leaving, "don't you have a shoebox full of about 15,000 green stamps under your bed somewhere?"

"What was he talking about?" Amos asked on our way home.

"Are you kidding me? You don't know?" I laughed. "He is looking for a payoff of fifteen thousand dollars to 'do what he can' to speed up our application. I know we have 500 thousand dollars of cash tied up in this project, but if we start with this kind of stuff, it will be like cancer and will never stop. Besides, it's wrong."

Amos nodded in agreement. We never paid a penny, and we finally did get our special permit. We just had to wait for it.

This project was called the Mill Creek Condominium Development. It was to be a 240-unit project with the first phase to be eighty-four units with a price range of $79,000-$110,000. We had hired a national marketing firm and, with the help of a national public-relations firm and our account manager, Constance Hubbell, we had coverage on the front page of the real-estate section of the *Boston Sunday Globe*. At the time, we were putting more units under agreement faster than any project in Greater Boston.

Then came Black Monday 1987! Many of our "young urban professional" clients were spread very thin and leveraged to the hilt; they had to recall their deposits. The project moved forward, and phase one was completed. However, since we had nonrecourse financing, and the bank wanted us to sign personally and immediately to keep the project running, we said, "No, thank you. Here are the keys, and by the way, you still owe us the balance of our developers' fee."

Amos and I were in a meeting with our environmental engineer, Dr. David Krutz. Amos had just told our receptionist, Judy, under no circumstances was she to disturb us during this meeting. She knocked on the door. "Amos," she said, "I have to see you now!."

"No!" Amos replied. "*No!*"

"I don't care if you fire me," she said. "I need to see you now!"

Amos went storming out of his office. He came back about five minutes later and motioned for me to come out. He asked me to follow him into the men's room.

"What's the matter?" I asked.

He held his finger up to his lips, "Shhhh!" As we entered the men's room, he handed me a subpoena. It was from the United States Federal Court Secret Grand Jury.

"What is this, and how come they called *you* out for this?"

"It was delivered by two FBI agents. One was an old college roommate of mine. They're investigating bribery in the City of Chelsea, Massachusetts—namely the Zoning Board of Appeals."

"Aha, the 15,000 Green Stamps guy."

He nodded. "My friend the agent said you should give him a call and talk to them before you speak with your attorney and you are not the target of the investigation."

"That's nice to know," I told Amos, "but are you crazy? I am not speaking to the FBI without speaking to an attorney first, whether he's your friend or not."

I called my lawyer, Joseph Kay, at B, D & G, and he suggested that I call Kathy Kregman, a constitutional attorney at the offices of D & C in Boston.

I learned during this experience that even though you have done nothing wrong, you need to have the very best in legal representation, and it will cost you a lot of money.

I also learned that even the most innocent of statements before a secret grand jury can be taken the wrong way, and you can be prosecuted over them if you are not protected properly. For that reason, Kathy obtained immunity for me from prosecution. An attorney told me, "You do not testify without immunity."

At the very last minute, we found out that the United States Attorney for the District of Massachusetts, Frank L McNamara, had been sworn in incorrectly. Therefore, as I testified, I had to take the Fifth Amendment until I obtained new properly administered immunity. Talk about being intimidated. I was finally granted new, properly administered immunity and, prior to my testimony, prepped by my attorney.

Your attorney cannot go into the secret grand jury room with you, but you do have the right to use the restroom. An attorney can wait for you in the hallway outside. If I was not sure of an answer, I had been told, I should take a "restroom break." During my testimony, I had to use the restroom four times. The US Attorney asked that it be put in the record that "Mr. Lazarus has a weak bladder"!

The irony of all of her questioning was that I was never asked even once about being asked for any payoffs or bribes either in the City of Chelsea or by Chelsea's chairman of the Board of Appeals. I suspect that she had gotten enough information from prior witnesses.

The Board of Appeals chairman was eventually indicted, and he did plead guilty.

There were two things that truly irritated me about the entire process. The first was that I did absolutely nothing wrong, and it cost me over $30,000 in legal fees to be represented. And second, when I got back to my office, I got a call from an unknown person who repeated to me verbatim everything I said to the "secret grand jury." Who was this "unknown person" and why did he call? I had no idea, but it was frightening, given that it was a *secret grand jury*.

***

Memories can haunt you. I decided I could no longer live in the house where Nancy and I had enjoyed so many happy times as a family for all those years. Constantly looking back made it difficult to move on. I sold the house, moving to a slightly smaller place in a development nearby. It came with a maintenance program, so I did not have to worry about gardening or upkeep.

My routine became going to work, coming home to be with Gregg, and calling Buffy and Jess frequently to check on them. I knew I had to pick up the pieces, look toward the future, and start a new chapter in my life. But I was unsure how to go about doing that. On one hand, I was very lonely, but on the other hand, the alternative to being lonely was kind of frightening for a man who had spent almost a quarter of a century married to the same woman.

Nonetheless, the parade of women started almost immediately. During *shivah*—the Jewish seven-day period of mourning—some women even wrote their phone numbers in the remembrance book when they came to pay their respects. Others offered to cook for me and "bring over some brisket" or whatever I wanted. In addition, I was the recipient of an endless list of the names and numbers of women who were friends of friends. I felt like fresh meat on the singles menu! I was more comfortable at first socializing with couples that both Nancy and I had known.

When the mourning period ended, I decided I needed to get away. I decided to go to Puerto Rico for a week or so. This turned out to be a huge mistake on several fronts. First of all, when I planned the trip, I was oblivious to the fact I would be away over Mother's Day, a difficult day for those who had just lost their mother. This was totally thoughtless on my part. It took its toll on my kids.

The second mistake was not realizing what I was getting into. Before I left, I stopped in the airport bookstore and picked up a book called *Sexual Static*, which was written primarily for women. The last three chapters, however, were a lecture for men on being suddenly single. "The mores and morals of the past have changed over the last twenty years", the book said. "Expect a whole new liberated world out there."

It was a good thing I read this book as preparation, because everything it predicted happened to me in Puerto Rico. From slightly forward women to sexually advancing women. It was like nothing I had ever experienced. After three days, I'd had enough. I said to myself, "I have to get out of here!"

I went to the concierge and said, "Get me a ticket to New York City."

I called my childhood friend, Jimmy Brokey. "Meet me in the city tonight at 8:30 p.m. at the Americana Hotel. I just need to go to dinner with you and talk."

Jimmy and I went to dinner and then out for a drink at some club. Lo and behold as *Sexual Static* had warned me, two women tried to pick me up. I began to wonder whether I had a sign on my back: "recently single." I just was not in the mood.

After this period of fear came a need to prove my virility. I was introduced to a woman and had a fling with her. Unbeknownst to me, she came into my house and measured the rooms to figure out where her furniture was going to fit. I wasn't there, but Gregg was. When I took off for a weekend jaunt with her, Gregg predicted to Jess, "Dad's going to dump this one."

Well, he was right.

For a while after that, I socialized mostly with old friends—couples Nancy and I had socialized with before. One Saturday night, Idelle and Lenny Marglow asked me to join them with Roberta and Bruce Twerl in the North End of Boston for an Italian dinner. While at dinner, the Twerls mentioned that they had bumped into Sharon Dames. They had asked her to join them, but she was busy.

I vaguely remembered hearing her name in the past. Since the Marglows had been trying unsuccessfully to fix me up for a while, I said, "I know, I know; she is getting a divorce. Give me her number, and I promise I will call her this week."

I really called just to be nice. Not so much because I was interested. When I went to pick her up for our first date, I was taken aback by her physical stature. They had not told me she was so short—almost the exact same height as Nancy. She was very attractive, beautifully dressed, and really had a great personality. More than that, I sensed there was something special about her, something warm and sincere.

That was the high point. At dinner, for some reason I spent what seemed like hours lecturing her on the fact that she had been separated for three years. It was time to get on with her life and finalize her divorce. Needless to say, it did not make for a wonderful evening.

About a month later, on a Saturday night at about 8:30 p.m., I was having dinner with the Marglows at a friend's home about an hour from where Sharon lived. Out of the blue, I asked Idelle for Sharon's phone number. I called Sharon and asked her if she wanted to go for an ice-cream cone or a drink. She thought for a few minutes but finally said yes.

We wound up going for a drink at the Marriott Hotel in Newton. She told me her daughter Loren was going off to college the next day. She was taking her, which was why she almost wasn't going to come. She explained she has two daughters: Loren was eighteen and Whitney was sixteen. We wound up dancing and talking until two in the morning.

A few dates later, I invited her to a grand-opening party for my Mill Creek Development. When we got there, coincidently, she said, "This is where my father had his former M & M Transportation trucking terminal." We saw each other nonstop from then on.

I asked Sharon to marry me a few months later. I told her I loved her so very much and wanted to spend the rest of my life with her. We were very excited, but at the same time we were realistic. We both sensed our two families were not going to blend together as seamlessly and happily as the Brady Bunch. That only happened on television. In fact, according to statistics, 60 percent of blended families failed in the first two or three years. We were determined that was not going to happen. We knew our marriage would probably be more difficult for my kids to accept than for hers, albeit still difficult for both.

Buffy was studying at a hospital in London for a semester. We decided to go to Europe for a vacation and stop there first to tell her about our plans. Buffy put on a good face, but I could tell she was conflicted, normal given the circumstances.

Our children ranged from sixteen to twenty-three. They were almost all out of the house. They were never forced to be together with the exception of an occasional holiday. They got along but did not develop any close relationships. Having spoken with some other families in blended family relationships, I've learned that some have gone as far as needing to have three different Christmas trees, so the various children could have their special Christmas ornaments displayed without over reaching into the other family's territory. I'm happy to say we never had that kind of hostility.

In fact, over the years, the most amazing thing has happened. Our grandchildren, even living in two different states, have developed a very special bond with us and each other through the use of technology: social media, texting, Instagram, Facebook, Skype, etc. They love being with each other and they constantly communicate, can't wait to get together again. You see, if you live long enough, anything can happen!

Sharon owned a house in Newton; I owned a house in Swampscott. We decided it would be best if we had a neutral house and should sell both houses. Sharon thought we should have a house where each of the kids would have his or her own room. I agreed, although in reality, we quickly realized the kids had been pretty much launched. They would not be coming back permanently. About a year later, we decided to move into the city and try urban living. We have been living in the city ever since, and that is almost twenty-seven years!

Chapter 4

CHALLENGES AND A
CHOSEN PROFESSION

Real-estate sales of new homes rose at a rate of almost 10-15 percent per year from 1982 through 1987. Then came the 1987 stock market crash. The Dow Jones Industrial Average dropped by 508 points (22.61 percent). The handwriting was on the wall. The real-estate market was going to change dramatically. Again, I needed a new vocation.

Although I went through a very difficult personal financial crisis after the meltdown of the real-estate market, I put on my track shoes and kept running. It was the only thing I knew how to do. I invested in the first franchise ever sold for Boston Chicken and had the area-development rights for the state of Connecticut. Boston Chicken was a chain founded in Newton, Massachusetts, in December 1985 that specialized in rotisserie chicken as well as a variety of side dishes. At first it seemed like a brilliant investment. The company was an immediate success and grew rapidly, but unfortunately, it also raised a lot of debt in order to finance its expansion. While its rapid expansion allowed the company to create a steady stream of revenue from one-time development fees and increasing royalties, it also meant higher interest rates on its development loans. That, in turn, caused the parent company, to file for bankruptcy.

I should have listened to my senior-year pharmacy professor, Dr. Raubenheimer who said, "A partnership is a dangerous ship to sail on." Every business venture I have been a part of that has been a partnership has somehow not worked out well for me. When I have been captain of my own ship and have been solely responsible for it, there has been a successful journey from port to port.

***

At the time, Jess had graduated from Boston University and moved to San Diego to work as a stockbroker in a small brokerage firm. Buffy was about to graduate from BU. Gregg, the only one of my children still living at home; had a part-time job working in a convenience store/sub shop. One day, he cut his hand badly on a slicing machine. I got a call from the Swampscott Police that they were taking him to Salem Hospital. I was close by and rushed so fast I arrived before the ambulance. When they brought him in on the stretcher, my heart stopped for a second. They had his body totally covered with a sheet.

My heart went back to beating when his head popped up.

Fortunately, Dr. Samuel Seminor, a plastic surgeon I knew, happened to be in the hospital at the time. He came right down to the emergency room, and he worked on Gregg for two hours. It turned out Gregg was a very lucky young man. He almost lost his hand, but instead wound up with a little scarring and very little nerve damage.

Gregg had grown into a very sensitive and caring person. When he received a substantial settlement from that injury, he ran out to buy his brother, sister, and me expensive gifts with the money. My gift was an Ebel watch with an inscription on the back, which read, "The Best of Times is yet to Come!"

I was touched but also confused, not knowing what exactly he meant by the inscription. I was also concerned, because the watch was too expensive and emblematic of some grandiose behavior Gregg had been exhibiting of late. If he bought someone a gift, it had to be the most expensive. If he went out to dinner, he had to take large groups of friends and treat. Often these "big shot" statements were followed by periods of anxiety. I wanted him to talk to someone, to see a therapist, but he refused.

You never know where life will take you. I had no idea what I was going to do after leaving the real-estate business and Boston Chicken in 1990. I did not know where to turn or what field of endeavor would be the next chapter of my business life. What would be the next door to open? I was sure I would find my way. I am not so sure that my wife, Sharon, had the same confidence I did. However, she kept her chin high and did a great job of disguising her anxiety.

Paramount to me in an innermost burning emotion that has always made me feel good about myself is my ability to help people in any way I can—whether it means being a shoulder for people to cry on, an ear that will listen, a person who can be used as a reference, help to find a doctor, or as former pharmacist who might find someone the right medication, or even just someone who can help secure a dinner reservation. I guess that's why in some circles I've earned the nickname, "Concierge." I have also earned a title of endearment from many friends, colleagues and clients of being known as everyone's uncle, aka Uncle Harvey.

How could I find a profession that took advantage of that drive?

As an entrepreneur, I always had an interest in life insurance and health insurance. I wondered whether this might be the right profession for me. I decided I would self-study to get licensed for life and health insurance. I went online and got two books on the subject and took the exam three weeks later, passing on my first try. I was licensed for both life and health insurance in the Commonwealth of Massachusetts. Little did I know then that the learning process in this wonderful profession would be continual and never-ending. I had just begun.

I got a job with the National Association for the Self Employed, selling what they said was health insurance. At the age of forty-eight, I was excited to even get a job. They paid weekly, and I sold a lot of policies. But soon enough, I came home and said to my wife, "I can't do this anymore. My clients think they are buying regular health insurance, but it is really just catastrophic health insurance." I didn't think they were intentionally deceiving people, but I also didn't think people understood they weren't getting what they thought they were. Either way, I didn't want to be part of it.

In his book, *Carry the Fire,* Rabbi Baruch HaLevi tells an anecdote about a time he was searching for direction in his life. He was at a crossroads, trying to decide whether to go in the direction of Buddhist spirituality by studying at the Naropa Institute in Boulder, Colorado, or to turn instead to Jewish spirituality by enrolling in rabbinical school at the University of Judaism in Los Angeles—two radically different choices.

He was waiting at the Denver airport, having just visited the Naropa Institute, exhausted and uncertain about what to do. When he looked up, he found Aryeh Azriel, the rabbi from the reform synagogue he'd attended as a teenager, standing in front of him. On his way to catch a flight, Aryeh hugged him and told him, before hearing the whole story about his dilemma, that he was going to become a rabbi. The rabbi invited HaLevi to come and shadow him in his work. Because it was Aryeh, who had shown an interest in him in his youth and because of the auspicious timing, Baruch HaLevi took notice. He became a rabbi. (He says in retrospect, he is grateful the Dalai Lama wasn't running to catch a plane that fateful day.) Here is a quote from the book:

> I had always marveled over the divinity of that encounter. Since then, I have seen this scenario, though far less obvious and dramatic, play out in a thousand different ways. Constantly, we are impacting one another, crossing in and out of each other's lives at hundreds or thousands of these intersections all day long. Some of the connections are blaringly obvious, and yet others are seemingly insignificant. So the question arises: are we simply ants marching through our lives with no ultimate purpose, no deeper connection than physically bumping into one another as we mindlessly go about our business; or is there something more?

The morning after deciding I couldn't stay at the National Association for the Self Employed any longer, I went off to change my bank account at the office for Union Central Life. I just happened to bump into the head of recruiting for the general agency for Union Central Life in Boston, whom I happened to know. He asked me what I was doing, and when I explained, he invited me to come to work for them. He said they had great training and a subsidy program that paid a new agent a salary while he was learning the business, since to work just on commissions was not viable at the beginning. After taking the typical psychological test that day, I was hired.

My "training" first consisted of having to make a list of all my family and friends and contact them to tell them I was selling life insurance. I immediately said absolutely not. I knew the attrition rate for agents entering the profession was so high that only 20 percent made it past the third year. Not very good odds. I made a commitment to myself, I would not solicit any family or friends for three years, I would only sell to any of them if they came to me.

The next part of the training consisted of handing me the yellow pages and a phone script. I was in the office at 5:30 a.m. and left at 7:00 p.m. at night. I figured if I found a business owner in at 5:30 in the morning, he was a hard-working individual and I might have a chance to speak with him, not having to deal with a gatekeeper answering the telephone. I worked my way out of the subsidy contract in less than six months.

I felt I had to find a way to be different from other insurance agents. As a young man, I had been an advocate of buying term insurance and investing the rest. However, I never got around to investing the rest! I had a great insurance adviser in those days, but I never took his advice. (If I had, I was sure I would have been in better financial shape). Why hadn't I? What did people hate about insurance salespeople? All those who had called on me had always made things appear so complicated, with mounds of paper and confusing ledgers. I thought if I could keep concepts simple and was honest with people, I could probably succeed at writing a lot of insurance policies. I decided that would be my mantra: keep it simple and be honest.

My own experience of lacking a life-insurance policy on my wife at the time of her death gave me another way to relate to people in a way that other insurance professionals could not. My experience with my wife's suicide was invaluable. There had been so many signs I could have recognized, had I known. Changes in eating habits, loss of weight, change of personality, changes of social plans, and so many others signs that haunt me to this day. Even the fact that she had post-partum depression after our first son was born (which I'm sure was never told to any therapist) was significant. When expressing myself to prospective clients I had a different way in, an invaluable tool that others did not. Perhaps if I'd had a life-insurance policy on Nancy, I would have been able to weather the storm of the real-estate fiasco of 1987-1988 differently.

Of course, it is always easier to look at things in hindsight, but when I did an estate plan for young couples, I pretty much insisted the husband had coverage for his wife, whether she worked in or outside the home. It was so important. Who would be there to take care of the children? Who would be there to babysit and to cook the meals? Who would be there when the husband was out trying to get his life back together?

Though I kept things simple in a presentation, it did not mean that I did not have the ability to analyze and prepare sophisticated estate-planning proposals. I always had all of the backup ledgers and mounds of paperwork to support my simple presentations. However, if my clients could understand the *concept*, the numbers and support documentation were the easiest part of the presentation. Over the years, this simple approach has proven to be the biggest asset to my practice.

I was selling myself by being me—being honest with people, listening, and giving people what they wanted to satisfy their needs. It was not about me; it was about them. Hearing people is vastly different from listening to people. Communicating with people is the art of creating relationships. As I said in my short biographical card that I presented to prospects and clients,

> *I speak with sincerity and candor, and my promise and commitment to you, my clients, is that I will listen and respond to your needs.*

The first step in a true relationship is communicating with openness and frankness between them and me. I have never wavered from that point. The only things that have changed over time was the products I had to sell and the solutions for problems that arose.

Within a year I was recruited by a larger, higher-rated carrier for a significant bonus. The carrier was Connecticut Mutual Life. I was mentored by an individual who had been in the business for about twenty years and whose practice was primarily in the area of investments.

My former bookkeeper from the book business called me. She told me that her masseuse mentioned that one of her clients needed help with insurance. Could her boss help them out?

This was my first referral. The people I was referred to, Donna and Vinnie Bono, lived in Everett, Massachusetts. On a cold, Tuesday night in December at 7:00 p.m., I went to see them. They were delightful. Vinnie had worked for Gillette as a machinist since he was sixteen years old. As I was completing my fact-finder and getting to know more about their wants and desires, I determined they needed a considerable amount of help.

They wanted to sell their home, move, build a new house. They needed life insurance. However, his annual income at the time was only forty-two thousand dollars.

Where, I asked myself, *is the money going to come from?*

"'I think this is worth something," Donna said, handing me a piece of paper as I was walking out the door.

Well, it certainly was! It was his Gillette Savings Plan statement, with a current value of $648,000. I told them I would get back to them in a few days.

Upon my return to the office, I told my mentor what I'd discovered. He said Donna and Vinnie were perfect candidates for a 72t(2) election.

What is that? I wondered. After some research, I became a "maven" on 72t(2) elections. A 72t(2) election was a way to withdraw funds from an IRA or a 401k prior to the age of fifty-nine and a half without a penalty under that section of the IRS tax code, providing the money was taken in equal, periodic payments for at least five years or until the age of fifty-nine and a half, whichever was longer.

This, I realized, could be a very useful planning tool.

The true moral of this story is, as so often attributed to Albert Einstein, but never been authenticated: "Compound interest is the eighth wonder of the world. He, who understands it, earns it ... he who doesn't ... pays it." Vinnie Bono had 10 percent of his pay taken out each week from the time he started working until the day he retired.

Subsequently, due to my previous real-estate background, I helped them get out of a bad real-estate deal they had on a piece of land. I helped them acquire a piece of property to build a home in Middleton. I sent them to an estate-planning attorney as well as a real-estate attorney and had them purchase some life insurance for Vinnie.

Donna and Vinnie Bono became my referral source for practically the entire machine shop and part of the management team of the South Boston Gillette facility. Many of my most loyal and trusted clients for the next twenty years—the McGarths, the Marbles, the Cugnis, J. Mancuso, B. Reichle, and many others—came out of that cold December meeting.

The first of the Bonos' referrals led me to their best friends, Bob and Kathy Daly. Bob was in management at Gillette and originally from South Boston. At our first meeting, sitting in their dining room, I gathered all kinds of personal information and completed a risk-tolerance questionnaire. I told them it did not matter how smart I was, that this was a trust business and they had to be comfortable with me. I had certain expectations of my clients. I gave them information about my experience and personal background.

Bob, however, was extremely skeptical, not only of what I had to say but of his trust in me and in any financial planner. "My South Boston upbringing has taught me not to trust anyone," he told me. "I have worked very hard to earn and save what I have accumulated over these many years. I am not sure I really believe the true honesty that you portray actually exists."

How's that for a challenge?

I talked about the back-and-forth I expected from my clients—I could not read minds, so at every stage they had to be upfront with me about exactly how they felt. If they had something on their minds, I wanted them to let me know, good or bad. If I asked them to read something, telling them it was important information, I expected them to read it. I told my clients we were dealing with their money and they had a responsibility to themselves to take an active part in the planning process.

I worked with Kathy and Bob to create a diversified retirement plan and helped to maximize his pension through the use of some permanent life insurance. I told them they had not gotten here overnight and the implementation of the plan would not take place overnight. During the first two years, we would meet every six months. After that, we would meet every June, after their return from Florida.

We put the plan into place and monitored its progress. I encouraged Bob, as I do with all of my clients, to call me with questions at any time. I gave him my cell phone number as well as my office number. I explained what would make me different from any other financial-services person was the service they would get from me and my assistant. "If there's a question that's important to you," I told them both, "then it is important for me to get you the answer. I may not be able to get you the answer immediately, but I will guarantee I will get it to you within twenty-four hours."

It took some effort, but that's how I overcame Bob's "South Boston distrust."

Additional referrals from that Gillette resource led me to the head of sports marketing for Gillette North America, Jim Ell. A marketing promotion sponsored by Gillette at the Super

Bowl was to have a contestants stand at the fifty-yard line and throw a football. Whoever was able to get it through the hole in a tire hanging from the goalpost would win a million-dollar annuity. I got to write the annuity. You never know where things in life will take you from a cold night in December! You also never know what money will do to someone. I learned shortly after the first payment was released to the winner of the one-million dollar annuity that his wife filed for divorce. Money can change a person's life, and it's not always for the better.

When I started out in the profession I didn't really understand "life insurance." I knew I was selling a product that would pay someone in the unlikely or premature death of a loved one, but I really didn't understand the impact insurance could have on someone's life. That came gradually, with learning experiences—like the one I had during my very first year in the business.

I went to see a young, hotshot software entrepreneur and his wife in Waltham. At the end of our meeting, he agreed to purchase a twenty-year-level term-insurance policy. I explained to him if he gave me a check for $120 to bind the application, he would be covered even though he had not yet been approved by the company. This would mean, basically free insurance for him during the underwriting process. He refused.

His wife said, "Don't move! Wait a minute!" She ran upstairs, got out her checkbook, and asked me to whom the check should be made payable. Two weeks later, he and his two partners were on a business trip, and their private jet crashed. The insurance carrier paid out one million dollars on her $120 check within three weeks after his death. When I went to pay the condolence call, the widow came up to me and said, "Thank you. If it weren't for you, I would be out in the streets and wouldn't know what to do."

That moment taught me what the profession is all about. There is nothing that impacts a new agent as much as delivering his first death-claim check. The more I learned, the more fervent I felt about how important life insurance was, and the stronger my argument became.

Life insurance is not *about* you, the person taking it out, or *for* you—you will be dead! You won't care! However, your wife, kids, and perhaps your parents, they will care. Who will take care of them? Who will provide the housing, clothing, food, and shelter for those you love? Who will pay for your children's college educations? Granted, you may not want your wife to be the richest widow on the street, but you probably want her to be comfortable and to live the same lifestyle she is accustomed to. Who will take care of your aging parents?

If you have a business, have you given any thought to what happens to that business if something happens to you? Who would take over the business? Who is capable of taking over the business? Your spouse? One of your children? A trusted employee? Will the business have to be sold? Or even worse, is the business sellable? Are you so busy working *in* your business that you can't take the time to work *on* your business? Are you so busy that you can't take the time to make a list of all the things your husband or wife needs to know in case something happens to you?

Very often when meeting with clients and gathering the very basic information about them and their families, I would ask, "What is the most valuable asset you own?"

Invariably they would stop and think and come back with an answer like "my home" or "my 401k" or "my stock portfolio."

"*Wrong!*" I tell them time and again. Your most valuable asset is your ability to earn a living." Most of them had never thought about it in that way.

I then discuss with them the necessity to insure that asset. "Would you rather insure a golden egg or the goose that lays the golden egg?"

They then began to see the picture more clearly.

One incident occurred in my early years in life insurance that drove home that issue. I met an attorney who had been convinced by an old college roommate to give up his law practice in Connecticut and move to Boston to become CEO of his roommate's printing company; he would have a 33 percent-equity position in the company.

I was handling the group's health insurance at the time, and I asked this new CEO if I could meet with him to discuss the company's buy/sell agreements and his personal insurance needs. We agreed a priority for the business would be to develop buy/sell agreements for the partners initially and funding the agreements partially with some low-cost term insurance. I referred him to a local, renowned estate-planning attorney.

We subsequently met at his home to discuss some basic estate planning for him and his wife and future child. I suggested at that time the most pressing issue for him would be to obtain some disability-income coverage. As with most clients, he hemmed and hawed about spending additional money on insurance.

I reminded him of what he was spending on car insurance every year, even though at the end of the year he hoped he would not get into any accidents. Thus, he would not get any return on the investment.

The estate-planning attorney reaffirmed the need for him to have disability-income insurance, and he called me back for a second meeting. "I finally get it," he said and agreed to purchase the maximum amount of coverage he qualified for based on his current salary. He was approved for a policy with a true own-occupation rider, cost-of-living rider, lifetime-benefits rider, residual-benefits rider, and guaranteed-insurability rider.

Two years later he realized, of his two partners, one was an alcoholic and the other was a drug addict. This caused unbelievable stress. Three years later, he had a nervous breakdown and was out on permanent disability. The company subsequently went out of business. After a prolonged period, the client finally was able to return to work, but he was extremely grateful to have had the disability insurance when he needed it.

Chapter 5

THE HOME FRONT

After graduating from Boston University, Jess got married to a television anchor who was working in Baltimore. They subsequently moved to Boston, then Detroit, and finally divorced while living there. In talking to me about his divorce, Jess said, when he was a kid and went to the court deposition with me, he learned that you had to keep going no matter what adversity you faced. "You taught me to keep your chin up and keep going forward." Jess sought a career in sales in the real-estate and the insurance industries.

After graduation, Buffy moved to New York City. Her first job was as an internal marketing sales representative with Lancôme, she then worked as a public-relations person for a small PR firm before deciding upon a complete career change: she became a pharmaceutical representative for Merck & Co. for several years. Then she met and married the man of her dreams.

Both Buffy and Jess shared their concerns with me about their younger brother. From the time of his mother's death,

Gregg was the one who always seemed to live on the edge, pushing the envelope. After high school, he went to the University of Tampa for one year. Deciding he didn't like the school or Tampa very much, he transferred to Johnson and Wales University in Providence, Rhode Island, where he majored in restaurant management.

When he was in his first year, Gregg's hair stylist talked him into participating in a credit-card scam. Gregg and his friends who had credit cards with high limits were buying goods on the cards. The kid with the credit card would then report the credit card as stolen. I did not learn about this until Gregg took the caper one step further, which resulted in dire consequences.

I was in my office at Connecticut Mutual in Waltham one Friday afternoon, when he called me, crying. "Dad, I need your help." He said, "You have to come down to the Swansea police station and bail me out!"

"What is wrong? What did you do?"

"I can't talk. Just come."

I didn't even know the location of the Swansea police station. I had to call them from my car to find out how to get there, and then I asked what Gregg had done. They told me his car was being used to transport stolen goods. I called a friend and said I needed to have a criminal lawyer meet me at the Swansea police station. This friend arranged to get me the former district attorney for the Taunton District Court, where the case would be heard. He represented Gregg and was able to get him a suspended sentence without prejudice—on the condition he stay out of trouble for one year afterward. He did stay out of trouble with the law, but there are other kinds of trouble.

When he graduated from Johnson and Wales, he moved to New York City. Gregg took a job working as a manager in the food-service department of Lufthansa Airlines, overseeing the preparation of the meals served to first-class passengers. He did quite well and was promoted. Gregg excelled at motivating the workers beneath him. However, he did not feel fulfilled, he said. He began having panic attacks, calling me in tears saying, "I don't know what to do with my life!"

He decided to try the insurance and investment business next. He was hired by AXA Financial. Gregg had no problem with the insurance exam and, much to his delight (and everyone else's surprise), he passed his series 7 exam on the first try. But this is a very tough business to break into. Although I tried to help him and even went to New York to go out on appointments with him, he was not willing to give it enough time and effort.

"Now that you're an adult," I said to him one day when we were in a New York taxi together, "how about telling me some of the things you did as a teenager."

"Oh, Dad, you don't want to know," he said. "I did it all."

This chilled me, because his siblings had alluded to this fact. They worried he was doing drugs. We all became concerned from time to time about his manic behavior. He worked out excessively. We could tell by looking at him that he was doing steroids. This, I thought, might be due to his self-consciousness about being short—that adding bulk to his body made him feel bigger.

Finally, after deciding that insurance and investment was not a career path for him, he moved to Florida. Gregg chose to go into business for himself as a mortgage broker. He seemed to be doing better. We all breathed a sigh of relief when, fifteen years after Nancy's death, he finally consented to regularly seeing a therapist.

Chapter 6

Taking Care of Others Sometimes Means Difficult Decisions

Kathy and Peter, who had been clients for a fairly long time, came in to see me for additional financial planning. Peter had just seen his company's stock options increase in value significantly, to the tune of approximately $600,000 dollars, and wanted to take some of those profits. He still had a large a number of additional options left, with more to be given to him that year. They were both forty-six years of age, with significant time until retirement. After we talked about their investment goals, risk tolerance, objectives, and retirement goals, we moved on to their estate-planning needs.

"Very often I might ask or say things you might not want to hear," I told them as we began. "But it is my obligation to say it like it is and ask certain things. Do I have your permission to go forward?"

They said yes.

Taking care of Kathy's needs was a rather simple matter. Peter, on the other hand, was a different story. They both agreed that we needed to get him some additional, permanent life-insurance coverage. We completed the application without any difficulty. Since I had first met with them, however, I noticed Peter had gained a significant amount of weight. In fact, he had become morbidly obese. At the risk of potentially losing the client, but telling the truth, as I always do, I asked, "Peter, do you want to be around with Kathy to see your son Bobby grow up and go to college?"

"Of course I do."

"Then I think you're going to have to take steps to get healthier, namely to lose weight. You know I used to be forty-plus pounds overweight. I lost that weight using a liquid diet suggested by my doctor to kick-start things, losing weight quickly. Then I changed my eating habits and began an exercise program at least three times a week. You don't have to run. Just walk on a treadmill for forty-five minutes, and you will see the pounds really start to drop.

"I'm telling you this because I care about you," I told Peter. "I did it for me, because I wanted to be around for my grandchildren. I want you to do it for yourself to be there for your son and, God willing, for your grandchildren too."

They could have fired me, but I am pleased to report that instead, Peter chose to take my advice. He dieted, exercised, and lost weight. Even more, he thanked me for calling him on it. Peter was motivated on his own. He just needed someone to give him the right motivation and a little push. I knew I was taking a risk. But it was more important to me to save his life than to make a sale.

Another client posed a more difficult decision. When I was selling group health insurance I worked with a large national corporation. I dealt with the vice president of human resources, who had recently moved to Boston from Kansas City. She did not know anyone in the area. My wife and I became socially friendly with her and her significant other.

Two years later, she got a new position as assistant dean at a prestigious university graduate school of business in Washington DC. It was a very high-pressure position requiring her specialized skills to help keep the school in its esteemed ranking among business schools in the country.

The following summer, when she invited us to spend a long weekend at their summer residence along the Virginia coast, she asked me to go for a walk on the beach. She told me she was adopting a little girl from China and asked if I would be the child's godfather.

I was shocked, surprised and, of course, honored. I said yes. She also told me her friend, who was African-American, was going to be the godmother.

"Wow," I told her, "a real United Nations of a family—Jewish godfather, African-American godmother, and Episcopalian parents for a Chinese child!"

She and her significant other, Gordon, were going to get married, but not until the adoption was finalized. The social-service agency told her that it would be easier for her if they waited. A few months later, she brought home the most beautiful baby, who was less than one year old.

She and Gordon decided to marry on the island of St. John. They asked my wife and me if we would be matron of honor and best man, their only two attendants. They got married on a sailboat in the bay—a justice of the peace, the bride and groom, my wife in her gown, her hair blowing in the breeze, bare feet, and me in my white dinner jacket, bow tie and bare feet.

Two years later, she came to Boston for a visit and stayed with us. I sensed something secretive and amiss. She behaved strangely. I thought I smelled alcohol on her breath at ten o'clock in the morning. I called her husband and asked if things were all right at home. He confided in me that there had been problems and she had been asked to take a medical leave by the university. She had been going to Alcoholic Anonymous meetings sporadically, but they were not really helping. He was at his wits' end. She had been caught driving under the influence with the baby in the car.

That was a red flag for me.

I confided to him that I had looked in her suitcase and found a bottle of vodka in a brown bag. I asked his permission to intervene. He gave me that permission. At this point, I called someone I knew to be a sponsor at AA. She warned me that if I did an intervention "you have to be prepared to give up that relationship, perhaps permanently, and at the very least for a number of years."

When my friend came home, I sat her down and had a heart-to-heart talk with her. "No bullshit … I want the truth. Tell me what's been going on. I will tell you what I did while you were out. I will tell you that if I ever catch you driving with your daughter in the car when you are not sober, I will call the police in Massachusetts. You will lose your daughter. Your husband will do the same in DC. Do you want to get better? If you do, you are going to call a facility right now and admit yourself. Here are the names of two facilities."

She made the call and admitted herself to a facility in Pennsylvania for thirty days with no visitors. Her husband was delighted. Her father was irate that I was the one who did the intervention, I was the one who took control. I think he was in denial. Perhaps he had always been the controlling person in her family.

I am happy to say she came through the treatment. She is now remarried and has been sober for fifteen years. We do have a relationship, albeit not what it was, but a cordial one.

My relationship with her former husband and my goddaughter is as strong as ever. She is a beautiful, very bright young lady. She just graduated from high school and will be attending Rutgers University. Her mother has done a very fine job in her upbringing.

These are positive stories. However, such honesty does not work with all clients.

There was the family with two sons and a daughter, who had been clients for a significant number of years. I worked with the parents for several months to help their attorney to complete their estate plan. This called for applying for ten million dollars of survivorship insurance. The mother had signed the application, and the father was due to sign the application right after Christmas. The day before Christmas, he went to buy his wife a car as a Christmas gift. He had a heart attack and passed away on the floor in the dealership.

Several months later, the mother called me to help get her financial house in order. At the time, she informed me she needed life insurance as well as needing to put a significant amount of funds away. She wanted them to grow tax-deferred and where she would be penalized for early withdrawal. The reason she needed to be penalized for early withdrawal, she said, was she knew one of her sons was a drug addict and an alcoholic and would plead with her for money. The other son, she thought, might be following the same path.

I suggested a better alternative might be to create a trust with a disinterested trustee. The trustee could dole out funds based on her criteria as set up in the trust.

She decided not to go that route.

Three to four months later, she informed me her son was doing much better. He told her he was in a rehab program and

"It's All About Life"

no longer on drugs or alcohol. Within six months of that date, she started to withdraw funds from her variable annuity and was paying huge surrender fees.

At the risk of losing the client, I told her she needed to seek professional help, not just for her son but for herself as well. I felt it was my professional responsibility to advise her in that fashion.

I lost the client.

In the end, her son forged her name on documents, drained her bank accounts and her investment accounts, wrote illegal prescriptions, and wound up in jail. His mother had a nervous breakdown and then got early onset dementia and Alzheimer's. The family lost almost everything.

Early on in my career, one of my biggest clients relied on me to handle all of his life insurance and investment needs. Previously, he had been raked over the coals by a less-than-scrupulous agent. He relied on me for monthly office visits to review all his mail related to his insurance and investments.

He was in need of additional second-to-die insurance for estate-planning purposes as well as additional insurance for the buy-sell agreement for his business. He had recently retained a new attorney, and the attorney asked me to obtain quotes for term insurance for their buy-sell coverage. He indicated that he only wanted two quotes, including one from a direct company (a company that only sold exclusively through their own agents) and would be difficult for me to get. I suspected trouble to be brewing.

After obtaining all of the necessary quotes (including a quote from the direct company, through a friend) for the term insurance and the second-to-die coverage, I received a call from his CPA. He told me he was sure I would get the business if I would take care of him on the side. I then took a calculated risk: I called the client and told him about the call. He could not believe it. I received a call from the attorney about a week later. I was told that I would no longer be servicing the client.

I subsequently called the client, writing a letter asking for a meeting. Had I done anything wrong? I never got a response. Subsequently, I have seen this person over the years, receiving a big hello as if nothing ever happened. However, to me, this was a very big disappointment, both personally and professionally.

There are times in my profession when you have to risk losing a client for the betterment of the family. As a professional, it is your obligation to act in your client's best interest, even when the client is not willing to acknowledge that it is his best interest. Then there are times you risk losing a client when the client refuses to come to his or her senses.

I recently received a call from a woman asking about her husband's life-insurance policy. After so many years of talking with clients and friends on the telephone, I have learned to sense when there is tension in their voices. Finally, I asked her, "What's wrong?"

"Paul and I have been separated for almost a year; we are living in two different houses," she told me. "We are getting a divorce, and it is going to be messy." She said she needed to come in to see me for a confidential meeting.

When we got together, she confided she had no one to talk to except me. I was the only confidant with whom she could share her very personal, emotional, and financial issues.

My first suggestion was to retain the very best divorce attorney she could find in the city. Her husband was an attorney, and she could be certain he would be using a very high-powered lawyer to represent him.

Sadly, she took a more convenient route, deciding to use an attorney she knew, who was not very experienced in divorce law. She called me three months later, crying hysterically. Her problems had multiplied. Her children were now going to her soon-to-be ex-husband's residence and experimenting with smoking pot.

I reiterated to her if she was going to call for advice and not take it, why call me in the first place? I gave her the name of two of the most powerful divorce attorneys I knew. I told her to use my name, along with another attorney's name as a referral source.

This time she listened. She made the decision to go forward with proper representation. She is now making progress.

CHAPTER 7

DEALING WITH LIFE'S TRAGEDIES

It was August 13, 2009. I was flying to meet Sharon at our friends' Dottie and Stuart Feinzig's home in Ventnor, New Jersey, near Atlantic City. Since Stuart and I could not get a direct flight, we had to fly to LaGuardia in New York and rent a car to drive to Ventnor.

We got off the plane from Boston, and at about ten a.m., I was standing in the rotunda of LaGuardia Airport, when my cell phone rang. When saw it was my son Jess calling. I picked up right away.

"Dad, are you sitting down?" he asked when I answered.

"No," I said. "Why? What's up?"

"Find some place to sit."

After I sat down in the nearest chair, Jess told me my son, Gregg—just thirty-eight years young—had committed suicide the night before.

I felt as though my body had undergone some sort of electric shock. I sat there, listening as he spoke, shaking my head. Jess was living in Vero Beach, Florida. He said there had been a knock on his door from two detectives from the Vero Beach Police Department. They asked him if he was Jess Lazarus and if he had a brother named Gregg Lazarus. When he said yes, he told me, he got a nauseous feeling in his stomach. He knew something terrible had happened.

The detectives told him Gregg had died. He had shot himself in the parking lot of the Boca Raton Police Department. They told Jess they suspected Gregg had done it there knowing his body would be found quickly. Gregg's body had been taken to the morgue. Jess could arrange to have a mortuary get the body after they did an autopsy. There were always autopsies in suicides. They told him he did not want to see the vehicle or Gregg; it was a gruesome sight.

After the police were done with their autopsy, Jess said he would take care of the arrangements with the mortuary. He said Gregg had left instructions he wanted to be cremated.

I sat there listening to Jess, staring at the people going back and forth, but seeing nothing. My initial reaction was shock, an empty void. Then came the tears. I turned to Stuart and said, "My son Gregg took his own life." He tried to console me as I cried. I called Sharon, and I called Buffy. We all cried together on the telephone. The shock was overwhelming.

When the shock began to wear off, all I could think of was. *Why?* Why would he take his own life? Why would he do something so extreme? Why couldn't he have called me or his brother or his sister to ask for help? *Why? Why? Why?*

Stuart was in shock too, but was very comforting. He asked what he could do to help, but of course, there was really nothing anyone could do.

I don't remember how much time elapsed before I pulled myself together. We went to get the rental car. Stuart drove us to his house in Ventnor for the weekend. All I could do in the car was cry and keep asking myself *why*.

I thought back to the last time I had spoken with Gregg ... it was probably a week before. He gave me his usual cheerful "Hello!" and told me things were going great. He said he had recently gotten predictable dialers for his company. This would allow his office people to reach more people. They could double the amount of mortgage prospects and, therefore, secure more mortgages per week. In Florida and in business for himself, he'd sounded upbeat ... but you could never tell with Gregg.

We stayed at the Feinzig's home for the weekend. Friends kept coming over to pay their condolences. I spent most of my time walking on the beach and the boardwalk, staring at the water and the waves trying to look for answers. None were to be found. Gradually, I realized none would ever be found.

One of my clients, a world-famous singer, was out of the country on tour. When he heard of Gregg's passing, he e-mailed me, saying he would be praying for him that evening, and he sang in Gregg's memory to the audience. The outpouring of expressions of sympathy and support from family, friends, and clients helped to soothe the pain somewhat, but it was always there.

Once Jess was able to pick up the ashes from the crematory and bring them to Boston, Buffy joined us at my house for three days. We consoled each other, hugged, and talked a lot about the good times, about Gregg's early years, the years when things were always good for us as a family. We talked about how much he was going to be missed, how loving and caring he was. We bemoaned the fact that he had never been able to really find himself. There was a lot of talk of "what if ..." and "if only ..." but we knew those were just wishes in hindsight, daydreams. *If only I were God, I could change the world.*

There was no funeral. Jess, Buffy, and I went to the cemetery where Nancy was buried. We spread his ashes with his mother. We each said something private. I repeated the Hebrew *kaddish*, the prayer of mourning for the dead.

We actually only sat shivah, the Jewish mourning period at my house for one day. Because we had many friends in the New York area, we also sat shivah for one day at Buffy's house in Westport, Connecticut. There were hundreds of calls and Legacy.com obituary postings for Gregg from all over the country. I could not believe how far and vast his friendships reached. Friendships were always very important to Gregg. After Nancy's death, friends became his extended family and his support system.

Gregg had a tattoo on his left shoulder of an eye with the word *Omerta*, which is the Italian mob saying for the "code of silence." About two weeks before Gregg's suicide, he and Jess had argued about Gregg's tattoo. Jess said he was too old. After Gregg's suicide, Jess took a picture of Gregg. He went to the same tattoo artist who had done Gregg's tattoo and had him replicate Gregg's eye on his left shoulder, putting the word Omerta as the eyebrow.

Jess says he now has Gregg looking over his shoulder all the time.

There is finality with death from sickness or an accident, along with a reason, an explanation that comes with that kind of a death. A death by suicide leaves so many unanswered questions. It affects many lives and in so many ways and for so many years. Suicide leaves scars, many of them irreparable. Suicide is an act of anger and selfishness, which most hurts those who loved the victim.

***

My wife, Sharon, and I go to Aspen, Colorado, for a ski vacation every year. In February of 2010, I went for a massage at the Aspen Sports Club. Since I was early for my massage appointment, I went into the hot tub. Another gentlemen in the hot tub asked me where was I from. I said that I was from Boston, and he said he was from Omaha. He then asked me if I knew of a town named Swampscott. I told him I had lived there for twenty-four years. He said, "My stepson just became the rabbi for a merged temple there. He goes by the name of Rabbi B."

Well, talk about six degrees of separation.

After my son Gregg died, I felt an inner need to connect to the temple where we had been members as a family—when the children were growing up, the synagogue where Gregg was a Bar Mitzvah boy. That temple had recently merged with another temple in the area, and thus was born a new congregation known as Shirat Hayam. I called the rabbi there—Rabbi Baruch HaLevi, DMin, aka *Rabbi B,* and left a message that I wanted to meet with him.

When he called me back, I said, "Are you the rabbi whose mother and stepfather were in Aspen this past February?"

"How did you know that?" he asked.

"That," I said, "is for another time. I would like to come to speak with you about my son Gregg's passing."

"I know a significant amount about his passing," he told me. "I have counseled more people than you can count about it. My time is your time. When would you like to see me?"

Rabbi B has a doctorate degree in ministry with an emphasis in Jewish spirituality from the Graduate Theological Foundation of Oxford University. He is a passionate writer and an avid practitioner of yoga; plus he has written extensively on the subject of suicide. He has personally been involved with the subject since the age of fifteen when his grandmother (his father's mother) took her own life. In 2006, once again it happened, when his father took his own life.

I have read many of Rabbi B's writings, his blogs and weekly postings. One in particular on suicide, which I believe is a must-read for anyone who has had the unfortunate experience to have to deal with a suicide, is a book he has written, *Carrying The Fire: A Brokenhearted Son's Journey through Surviving Suicide*. All of his writings are available from his website at http://www.rabbib.com/category/blog/. His newest forthcoming book is called Spark Seekers: Mourning with Meaning; Living with Light.

Shortly after making contact, Rabbi B and I met and spent two hours together. They were extremely emotional for me, and yet very uplifting at the same time. I learned much about myself, about life, and more importantly, about the continuation of life—life must go on, no matter how difficult it may seem at the time. What God has planned for us all is that we must go on. As Rabbi B says, there is always a glimmer of sunshine in every day. As the days, weeks, and months go by, the days will get brighter. We must, he says, "carry the fire"—carry on the good things the person we mourn brought into this world.

"I will devote my life to entering other people's darkness," Rabbi B says in his book, "sitting with them, lighting their reality and showing them the real exit out of the darkness, not through suicide, not through other short cuts but through "the work"—love, compassion, goodness and forgiveness—the real stuff of life."

I too have counseled numerous families on suicide, for it is unlike any other form of death. I never realized the numbers of people who have been touched by suicide, either directly or indirectly, within their families, by colleagues or very close friends.

Suicide is much more prevalent than most people realize. The CDC (Centers for Disease Control and Prevention) keeps statistics on suicide and reports that 41,149 cases were reported in 2013. That is an average of one person ever 12.8 minutes! Furthermore, another amazing statistic is that suicide loss survivors, those most intimately affected by suicide is staggering. It is estimated that for every suicide 25 people are directly affected. According to the American Association of Suicidology there were over one million suicide loss survivors in 2013. Very likely, this is a much underreported statistic for a myriad of reasons. Many more deaths are suicides that have been reported as something else. It may be police indifference; it may be just reported as unknown causes.

Quite a number of my clients, unfortunately, have been touched by many forms of mental illness that have ended in suicide. People commit suicide for many reasons other than mental illness. It varies from culture to culture. Clients are always quite surprised when they see me show up at the funerals or wakes, since they know my family history. However, it is also therapeutic for me. It truly helps them to know they have someone to talk with who understands the pain and grief they are experiencing and can help explain what they are going through. Becoming aware of the process of mourning and the transformation they will face as the future unfolds, I have found to be very helpful during the healing process.

Chapter 8

BUILDING RELATIONSHIPS
MEANS EVERYTHING

Since that cold December evening when I met Donna and Vinnie Bono, they have moved and built two homes, a vacation home in Florida, and a significant seven-figure net worth. Donna lights candles for me in her church and sends me notes and cards for every holiday. They even, each year on the anniversary of Gregg's death, send me notes of remembrance telling me they know it must be a difficult day for me and wishing me well.

Kathy Daly and her husband, Bob (whose South Boston upbringing made him distrust me when we first met) recently told me, "You are the best thing that has ever happened to us. We would not be where we are today, living the lifestyle we live, if it were not for you. The best compliment we can give you is that we have sent our children to you to get the planning advice that will help them plan for their futures."

They have no idea how much that statement means to me. There is no amount of money that can repay me for those kind words of praise.

When I took the psychological exam given to all recruits at Connecticut Mutual back in 1992, I was told the results made them reluctant to hire me. Why? Because my test results indicated I would forgo a sale to develop a relationship. In the end, the general agent decided to hire me anyway. And today, "promote relationships and sales will follow" has become the industry mantra, as well it should.

From the very beginning, I have always provided my clients with my office phone number, my e-mail address, my home phone number (before we had cell phones), and now my cell phone number—along with my assistant's phone number and e-mail. I have instructed my clients I am available to them *24/7*.

If something is important to them, and they feel they need to reach me immediately, I want them to know they will hear back from me, if not instantaneously, within four hours. This kind of service is the differentiator between me and many other insurance and planning advisers. Most issues are not critical in nature. However, if contact removes a client's anxiety, it is worth it. It is the small things you can do for yourself and others that become so meaningful.

In business, if you are looking for the lowest price, you can always find a vendor who will sell you an item cheaper than someone else. However, cheaper does not always mean better. Service, I feel, is a more important quality than price. If you needed a favor, the lowest-price vendor might not be there when you need him. Service and relationships are the cornerstone in any business or profession. It has been the hallmark of most successful people. They surround themselves with professionals who take pride in providing exceptional customer service to their clients. I have been so fortunate in my business career and professional life to have cultivated such relationships.

I have made it a point to deal with people I know will help me give my clients the services they need. In 1991, the year I started in this profession, a young man named David Baime took over the franchise for APPS (American Para-Professional Services). I told David we both were getting started in this insurance business, and I promised to give him all of the insurance exams I ever needed. However, I expected only one thing in return. If I ever called and said I needed a favor, such as an exam done in a hurry or on a Saturday or Sunday, I expected him to provide that service. Over the past twenty-three years, we have both lived up to that commitment; our relationship has flourished with mutual respect for each other as we have grown.

Sometimes, when the relationship is a strong one, you get credit you don't entirely deserve. My father taught me many years ago, "Nothing is forever." Translating that, nothing in the investment world continues to go up in a straight line. With that in mind, in 2008, just before the major market meltdown, I sent my long list of clients from Gillette letters reminding them

I had managed their accounts for quite a long time. They all had done quite well over the years. It had now come to a point where my years of experience had led me to give them two choices. If they followed my advice, we would remain good friends and continue a long and loyal working relationship. If they did not, they would have to find a new financial adviser. My advice was they take at least 50 percent of their investable assets and put them into a safe, guaranteed account. I was very serious in what I wrote. I lost two of those clients. Those who stayed with me were glad that they did. Now all of these clients think I walk on water.

I was not clairvoyant; I was just following my father's advice and exercising good, old-fashioned "common sense."

In my opinion, the granddaddy of all relationship-building is Jim Ash. He founded Ash Brokerage in 1971 as an insurance broker providing a full line of products to the insurance-brokerage-agency community. Jim is considered to be one of its founding fathers. In 1999, Jim was named the Ernst & Young Entrepreneur of the Year in northern Indiana. He has held advisory-board positions providing guidance to more than ten insurance carriers. In 2013, he was name to the Junior Achievement Hall of Fame. Under his tutelage, Ash Brokerage has been named to "Best Places to Work" for the past seven out of eight consecutive years. Jim's primary focus has been, and continues to be, nurturing and developing relationships.

When he finally started his own brokerage business in Fort Wayne, Indiana, he found that, in order to grow the business, he needed to expand his geographic area to Chicago, Detroit, Indianapolis, and Cincinnati. His prospects said to him, "What have you got to offer me that I can't get from my existing sources?"

At this point, Jim realized that he needed to provide superior professional and personal service to his clients that no other brokerage agency provided. He developed software that had been unavailable in the insurance-brokerage industry for life- and health-insurance sales. Furthermore, he believed in nurturing relationships with young people and allowing them to flourish in their roles within the company. It was his philosophy that it was never about what was in it for Ash Brokerage. If you took care of the firm's clients correctly, all the rest would take care of Ash in the end. Jim's son calls him an *uplifter*. If people make mistakes, he helps them learn from their mistakes. He helps to make them better people. He now spends most of his time these days building friendships and relationships, which is his passion.

I met an insurance consultant named Marc Diamond of Insurance Consultants Associates, Avenel, New Jersey, quite by accident. Some twenty years ago, while I was the acting general agent for National Life of Vermont, I called a client of his who was a very famous women's clothing designer. Her assistant told me I had to call her insurance consultant. I called Marc, explained that if she was healthy, she was overpaying for her current policy, and she could save over $20,000 per year by rewriting her policy. He asked me to send him the information.

He called me back a few days later and asked why *wouldn't* she want to do this?

I told him this was a no-brainer—the old agent was getting paid renewal commissions on the annual increases of her current annually renewable policy.

Although I did not secure the new policy at the time, the following year, the clothing designer called my office for information on her policy. I told her that if I could come and see her, I would show her how I could save her over $26,000 per year. I would provide the information at that time. If not, I would give her the toll-free number for the home office.

Once again, she told me to call Marc Diamond, and once again, I called Marc. He told me he had an appointment in New York at their office the following week. Could I be there to make my presentation? He asked me to forward him the information in advance, and he would be sure it would get done.

After the meeting, at which she bought the new policy, we went for lunch. I went to pick up the check. Marc said, "I am sorry, but we need two separate checks."

I asked why; it was, after all, only a sandwich.

"I work for my clients, and I have to be very clear that I cannot take any compensation," he said. "Even lunch."

I was absolutely stunned. In all of my years in business and in this profession, I had never heard of someone with such high moral and ethical standards with their clients' interests at heart.

Since that very first meeting, we have had a wonderful and meaningful working relationship for over twenty years. Marc uses me not just to have his clients purchase insurance, but as a resource for information regarding life insurance and estate-planning issues, business buy-sell agreements, disability-income insurance and long-term-care insurance. Very often, we just chat about planning issues regarding intricate family issues, as many of his clients are family-owned businesses.

Relationships do require work. Whether in business or in friendship, you must constantly work on maintaining that close, sustaining bond. Take a relationship for granted, and it will diminish and wither away. Some relationships may even require professional help, through either business or personal counseling. Remember, there is no shame getting professional help, if needed.

It does not take very much to maintain a close continual bond. Just a short note, a card, or a quick call can let people know you care or are thinking of them. It can be so meaningful to the recipients. These small gestures will make both of you feel so good and your lives more meaningful. Personal experience has taught me it is certainly worth the effort. It pays off with large dividends.

Timing is also important in maintaining relationships. Rather than attempt to reason with someone in the heat of anger, it is best to calm down, step back, and let cooler heads prevail. I recently got a call from Joe, a client with whom I had developed a close professional and personal friendship. Joe was in great despair over an issue he had with his closest friend, Tom. An attorney, Joe had represented Tom in a major litigation case, which had just been settled for a substantial seven-figure amount.

The settlement agreement eliminated any payment to nonvoting shareholders.

Joe's wife was one of the nonvoting shareholders.

What upset Joe was Tom knew of this arrangement and had not disclosed it to Joe.

When Joe called me, he explained to me that he felt violated and disappointed that Tom would treat these shareholders, especially his wife, in such a manner after all their years of friendship. He was furious and extremely hurt.

I happened to also know Tom. I knew his personality. He was a rough and tough construction person who had worked hard and made it. He almost lost everything during this litigation. He was also a hot head. But underneath it all, he was a very sensitive, kind person. I suggested to Joe he not act in anger, but instead he let the deal go through. When it was over, he should take Tom out for a beer. "Put your arm around him and tell him that he is one of your very dearest of friends. However, there is something preying very heavy on your heart and you must get it off your chest. Tell him what it is. Also tell him that in no way will this affect your relationship, and speak your peace."

While Joe was contemplating my response, he called me back and told me that Tom had just called him and said, "You know, Joe, I've been thinking about what just happened, and I want you to know I would never let you get hurt!"

Sometimes, however, it seems as if nothing can repair a relationship—even one that has existed for fifty years. I have had one major friendship disappointment with a person who I had been friends with from the age of four to the age of fifty-four. Together we have shared many of life's ups and downs.

When experiencing that first-time-bachelor experience as a widower after Nancy's suicide and going a little crazy being besieged by women at the resort in Puerto Rico and needing to talk to someone, it was Jimmy I called.

When his daughter, who was going to college in Springfield, Massachusetts, joined a cult with a boyfriend, it was me he asked to help him kidnap her.

I said sure, and I readied myself to meet him at the airport with my truck and sneakers on, ready to go. However, rather than kidnap her, we hired a friend who was a retired state trooper to follow her to be sure she was okay. He finally got to her and gave her the money she needed to go back home to New Jersey.

We had always been there for each other.

First Nancy, then later Sharon and I, with our children, had always spent a couple of weeks sharing a rental house with Jimmy and Jean in Montauk, New York, in the summer. One summer, they decided they would like to rent the house for the entire month and that we should come for the last two weeks. As usual, we would share the cost. We agreed, saying it would be just fine; we invited our kids to join us during the last two weeks.

When we arrived, Jimmy and Jean informed us their children had been out to visit with them the week before.

"Isn't that great?" we responded.

While I was taking my first bite of dinner, Jean said, "Jimmy and I have decided we don't want any kids here the next two weeks."

At which time, I spit the food out of my mouth. "We have always had our children here," I protested. "We have paid for these two weeks and should be entitled to have whomever we wish!"

We stopped speaking for the remainder of the two weeks and, sad to say, have not really spoken since. Although I've tried to make amends: I called Jimmy and told him that I wanted to continue to have a relationship with him and, if he was also willing, to continue to be friends. However, I could not forgive what he said.

When that proved unsuccessful in resurrecting the friendship, I tried again the following summer. I asked the four of us to meet for breakfast, without pointing blame, to see if we could rekindle a relationship for the sake of me and Jimmy. However, I guess they felt too much emotional damage had been done.

On one hand, this is the story of a failed relationship, but on the other hand, I firmly believe most relationships can be resurrected, especially those that have a long history. From my perspective, if he were to change his mind, I would gladly meet him halfway. If he were to call me in the middle of the night and say he needed help, I would be there.

I recently attended a memorial service for a ninety-two-year-old gentleman named Caleb Loring Jr. I did not know him, but I did know his son. It was a very moving service in celebration of the life of this gentle and caring man. He was a man who cared for his family, children, grandchildren, his friends, and business associates. He was a mentor to many young business associates and a philanthropist who helped so many. He had a special place in his heart for the *USS Constitution* Museum, where he was chairman emeritus of the *Old Ironside* Museum.

At the memorial service, a story was told that struck me; it was about Caleb's true effect on people. A young man heard of a speech being given by someone from Fidelity Investments, and so he went to attend. When the man from Fidelity was done, he went up to him and asked if he had heard of his grandfather, Caleb Loring Jr. The man opened his wallet, took out a picture of his grandfather, and said, "I carry this with me every day. He mentored me as a young man, and I owe my success to him." Caleb personified the true spirit of caring for people.

There are so many people looking for a "Caleb" to be there for them. They just need to let the inner thoughts they have been harboring for so long get out to an unbiased, nonjudgmental party. They don't necessarily want answers, and they don't want to be judged. Be a consoling shoulder for them to cry on or an ear to be listening. It will make their day and yours. It will make you a better person and enrich your life. You may not have the answers to solve their problems or even answer their questions. However, you may be that person who steps in at the right moment in someone's life, when they need to be lifted out of depression or anxiety. Or you may be the person to help set their sail for their career in the right direction. Stop for a moment and think about it.

Chapter 9

LIFE LESSONS

**Being a good employer yields a big return on the
investment.**

Since I entered the life-insurance business I have had three
assistants. That's an average of more than eight years for each.
Tara Meyck was with me for nine and a half years. She
originally answered an ad for a job as a telephone receptionist.
I told her she was over-qualified. I asked her if she was
interested in being my executive assistant. I also told her if she
had something on her mind, come in and tell me, as I was not
a mind reader.

About a month after she started, she came in and told me
she could not continue because she had not been truthful on
her application. She had not graduated from college. She still
had to complete her senior year. She was a great assistant, and I
allowed her to continue working. After her one-year
anniversary, she enrolled in night school at Northeastern
University, completing her education, and graduated with a
major in mathematics and education. She also became fully

licensed for life and health insurance, as well as Series 7 General Securities, which certified her to buy and sell investments for others. She continued her education, becoming a certified financial planner. However, she always wanted to become a teacher, which she finally did after getting married and becoming the mother of two children.

Beisy Navarro, my current assistant, has worked full time since she was in high school and while attending Regis College, from which she graduated with honors. Beisy is fully licensed for life insurance and securities and has just become a junior partner in my practice to assure my clients continuity in the future.

I have always believed there should be mutual respect in an employee-employer relationship. I have told my assistants there is nothing I will ever ask them to do that I have not done myself. I have always asked them to take responsibility for making decisions. I have explained further I would never chastise them in public, nor would I ever tell them they should never do something *like that* again. Rather, I would suggest a better or different way to handle a task. This approach has served them and me extremely well over the years.

It is extremely important to maintain a professional and courteous environment within your entire office every single day. Always remember to say good morning or hello to the receptionist and to other administrative staff in the office. It will make their day and yours too. Treat others the way you like to be treated!

My experience with other companies further supports my belief that an employer who cares about his staff gets that care returned many times over. A hedge fund in New York wanted to provide a benefit to all of its employees by providing basic estate-planning documents for all of its employees, paid for by the firm. In fact, they made it mandatory for all employees to have at least a basic will in place as part of their employment contract with the firm.

The reason the firm made this both a free benefit and mandatory was that two of the principals had a friend who had recently died *intestate* (without a will), meaning he had no estate-planning documents in place. They saw how this tore the family apart and raised havoc, not only within the family but in legal costs and time in the New York court system to settle the person's estate.

I was asked to recommend three estate-planning attorneys to their in-house counsel from whom she would choose to prepare the documents for their employees. I was to be the liaison and available to all the employees should they desire to purchase life insurance or disability insurance, or they could use their own insurance agents. I selected two estate-planning attorneys from New York, along with Patricia Annino, JD, from Boston. They selected Patricia from Boston. Patricia and I go back as far as 1989, when she did some estate-planning work for a family member, before I entered this profession. Since then, we have developed a professional relationship. She is a nationally renowned estate-planning attorney with over thirty years of experience and the author of several books on the subject, including *Women & Money—A Practical Guide to Estate Planning* and *Women in Family Business—What Keeps You Up at Night* and *It's More than Money: Protect Your Legacy.*

We initially did group meetings with all employees, explaining what the firm was doing for them. Patricia explained the basics of estate planning, and I explained basic types of insurance. We then arranged individual meetings with all of the employees and their spouses. The firm paid for all of the estate-planning documents for the employees. Those included basic wills, trusts (if needed), health-care proxies, durable powers of attorney, and living wills for those who wished to have them.

Comments from the employees were absolutely incredible, such as "I have never worked for a company that cared so much for its employees" … "I always knew I needed to get this done but never made the time to do it" … and "I can't believe how great this is."

During one of these interviews, we met with an executive secretary, Rose Zhang, who said she and her husband owned a number of pieces of real estate in New Jersey. She indicated she was the primary breadwinner, and she said the real estate brought in a fair amount of income while her husband worked as the property manager. She purchased a one-million-dollar term life-insurance policy. I suggested she needed a two-million-dollar twenty-year-level term life insurance policy on her husband. He refused to pay for the term-insurance policy. She told him she would pay for the term policy out of her income.

She was terminated by the hedge fund in 2007. I maintained contact with her over the years, and in May of 2010, I received a call from her that her husband had died of lung cancer. She explained it was very quick, a matter of weeks from diagnosis to his death. I told her not to worry, that I would handle the claim; all I needed was to have her sign a form and send it back with a copy of the death certificate. At that time, she had two sons, ages nine and ten. I delivered a two-million-dollar check to her within seven days of my receiving the signed paperwork back.

We met and hugged with lots of tears and also the joy of knowing that her future and that of her sons' educations would be taken care of. She could not thank me enough for making sure, when we originally met, that she did the right thing for her family.

One of the other young men who attended those meetings had all of the documents prepared. However, he chose to purchase life insurance through a friend of his who had just gone into the profession. This was just fine, and he took my advice and purchased a two-million-dollar twenty-year term policy. In 2008, the company was going through "some re-engineering," as they say. In other words, they were handing out some major lay-offs. This young man thought he was about to lose his job and took his own life. Fortunately, he had taken care of his family and had all of the estate-planning documents in order. There was life insurance in place to take care of his wife and young son. The firm was so taken aback and shocked (ironically, he was *not* on the list of those to be cut), they asked me to recommend another New York attorney that I work with to probate his estate. The firm would pick up all charges.

Employee loyalty is not always won over by dollars. Quite often, it is achieved by management's showing it cares by offering extra benefits.

This hedge fund example not only shows what a company can do for its employees; it also underscores another life lesson.

Estate planning is not just for the wealthy: this is a necessity for everyone.

In fact, 61 percent of Americans, according to a 2013 Harris Survey, do not have the most basic estate-planning document—a will. There are very basic documents that everyone should have and that are not expensive to have produced by competent legal professionals.

This is especially important for women, who are often not as aware as they should be about their finances. I very often get calls from female clients who are in the midst of a divorce or are recent widows. I realize how many women lack the necessary financial information about their families. There are so many easy steps they can take to gain this knowledge, in the ordinary course of business. I'm not talking about steps in preparation for a marriage to break up, but rather just items they should know in case of an emergency:

- Make a list of who to call if something should happen to a spouse. This list should include your accountant, your attorney, and the location of the copies of wills, trusts, and other estate-planning documents.

- Where are the copies of your insurance policies? Who is your insurance agent, financial planner, investment adviser, or stockbroker?

- You should know where all the copies of the bank statements are kept, along with the investment statements.

- If you have a safe deposit box, are you a signer on that box, and where is the key?

These are all vital pieces of information. And by all means, ask the right questions! It is incumbent upon you, the client, to look at what you are purchasing and ask questions and make sure you understand what it is that you have purchased. You should not be embarrassed to ask lots of questions. It is your right, and it is the obligation of the agent to give you truthful and honest answers.

Most insurance salesmen are not trying to sell, but rather to protect.

Very often, prospects/clients think we are salesmen trying to make more money by selling larger premiums. Most good professionals are just trying to give good honest advice to protect their clients.

I was referred to a young man who was an options trader in New York; he wanted to see me for insurance planning. He and his wife had just had a baby boy, and he was earning over $600,000 per year and was age thirty-one. They agreed to purchase ten million dollars of life insurance. I convinced him, because of how essential his income was, that it was important for him to have individual, disability-income insurance in addition to the group coverage that his office provided. Based on his age and income, he qualified for a maximum-benefit-coverage amount of $20,000 per month. I suggested that we include a *true own-occupation* rider, a compound cost-of-living-adjustment rider, a residual rider, and because of his age, a lifetime benefit rider.

He and his wife agreed. I also suggested a very-low-cost catastrophic rider, which would cost only $220 more per year, and which, in the event of a horrific catastrophe such as loss of limb or loss of sight or hearing, it would pay him an additional $8,000 a month in benefits. I also explained that all of the benefits for disability income would be tax free, since he was using his own after-tax dollars to pay the premiums.

Both policies were issued as applied for. His disability-income policy was issued on February 23, 2011.

I got a call from him on the twenty-eighth of February, and he told me that he and his wife had talked things over and they both felt that they really did not need that much disability coverage. Would I please change the monthly benefit amount to $12,000 per month and remove all of the "fancy" riders.

I said, "Are you sure that is what you want to do?"

His response was affirmative.

I was sitting at my desk on March 15, 2011, at 2:30 in the afternoon, and I got a call from him. He said, "Harvey, I have a f__king brain tumor! It is not cancer," he said, "but it affects my hearing and sight. I will be out of work and may or may not be able to return to work … ever! I am going out to California to the most renowned specialist in the world for this type of tumor to have some form of radiosurgery—*cyber-knife*."

I told him not to worry; my prayers were with him, and I would notify the company. I sat at my desk and wept for about an hour. If only they had taken my advice.

On August 3, 2012, I received the following e-mail from him, which makes this wonderful profession of mine worth it all:

> *MetLife approved my full claim! Thank you so much for helping me protect and provide for my family during such a difficult time. It is nice to not have to worry about other issues in addition to all my health problems.*

It is important to give unselfishly back to the community.

My wife, Sharon, and I have been blessed to meet so many wonderful people who give so tirelessly and timelessly of themselves to others. People like Sparky and Jake Kennedy. They started Christmas in the City, a 501-3c, charity in 1989, from their home. Its mission was to provide a holiday party and gifts from their "wish lists" for children from homeless shelters in the Greater Boston area. The party has grown from 165 children the first year to over 5,000 homeless children and 2,000 parents from homeless shelters this year. In addition, it provides gifts for another 17,000 children in homeless shelters who do not make it to the party. It is accomplished by an all-volunteer staff. Not one single paid staff member. What an incredible undertaking from the hearts of all involved.

Your future depends on you and only you.

My most recent affiliation has been with Baystate Financial Services. Managing Partner Dave Porter had been trying to recruit me for a number of years. "Why don't you come over here?" he kept saying. "We have a great culture and great resources that will support you and your practice." He said, "You're a perfect fit, and we need a real-life guy."

I must say that Dave was right. Baystate has been the right place for me. Furthermore, of all of the general agents that I have worked for, he is the most honest and has the highest moral and ethical character. Whatever he says he will do, he does—and more. However, he expects that you will do your part as well. He will hold you *accountable*.

He recently coauthored a book with Linda Galindo entitled *Where Winners Live*. He and I both believe strongly in personal accountability, that each of us must first be accountable to ourselves for our successes and our failures. As he so vividly points out, "Only we control our destiny. Personal accountability becomes a way of life for those who wish to be successful."

Do not be afraid to face life's challenges head on!

I hope you have learned something from reading this book, from my own life stories, and from those of my clients, friends, and strangers. We have all gone through various forms of struggle, tragedies, disappointments, medical difficulties, but for the most part, we have all come through them with heads held high. In most cases, we are better for enduring those life struggles and experiences. You must always look forward to a better day and be positive. If you have that constant burn of fire in your belly to do better for yourself, your family, and your community, things have a way of working out.

My dad used to say, "No one said life would be easy, but no one said it would be this hard either." Always take the challenge. That does not necessarily mean you must take risks. However, if you decide you want to take a risk, do it with open eyes, and educate yourself first. Be sure you are armed with the ammunition of education. This will give you a distinct advantage as you move forward and enter that next chapter of your life. I wish you each the best in that chapter.

There comes a time in one's life when a person starts to look at the world differently. You may even call it an epiphany. I would rather call it maturity. It is a time in a person's life when he reaches that age when things start to come together, and he begins to see things from a totally different perspective. Although he has been gradually maturing and has added responsibilities to his life, he begins to understand life has much more meaning than just waking up in the morning and going to work, going for drinks with friends, going to sleep, and starting the same routine over again the next day.

When is that time or date? It is so different for each and every one of us. However, it is there for all of us, no matter how subtle it may be. You might not recognize it immediately, but if you think back and are honest with yourself, you probably will remember when it started for you. What are the things and the life events that shape our lives? Some were for the better and some were for the worse. But they are all there.

FAVORITE QUOTES

FROM MY LIFE'S EXPERIENCES

&

ONE FOR GOOD MEASURE

You can take all of your degrees and put them in a brown paper bag; just give me good old common sense.

—Grandma Silver, my maternal grandmother

I don't want to be a millionaire; I just want to live like one.

—Charles Lazarus, my dad

Rich or poor, it's good to have money!!!

—Charles Lazarus, my dad

Sometimes it's better to be lucky than smart!!!

—Yours truly

What is your biggest asset? Your ability to earn a living.

—Yours truly

A partnership is a dangerous ship to sail on.

—Professor Raubenheimer, Northeastern University,

College of Pharmacy

Is it better to insure the goose that lays the golden egg or the golden egg?

—Yours truly

Many people have deep pockets and short arms.

—Yours truly

You can't polish a sneaker.

—Yours truly

Don't lecture me until you stand in my shoes!

—Yours truly

Something good will happen today.

—Dr. David Danforth

The One for Good Measure

Tomorrow will be a better day.

—Miriam Lazarus, my mom

ABOUT THE AUTHOR

Harvey Lazarus is married to Sharon, his wife of twenty-six years, and lives in Boston. He has two wonderful, grown children: Jessie, of Miami, Florida, and Lauryn, along with her husband, of Westport, Connecticut; and is blessed with two beautiful, fantastic grandchildren. He also has two great stepdaughters, Loren (and her husband), of San Francisco, California, and Whitney (and her husband), of Wellesley, Massachusetts, and is blessed with another four fabulous grandchildren.

He has a bachelor of science degree from the College of Pharmacy, Northeastern University, and a master's degree in business administration from Suffolk University's Graduate School of Management. A licensed life and health agent, he is general securities licensed with New England Securities. He is also a Massachusetts licensed insurance adviser and consultant and a life member of the Million Dollar Round Table. Harvey is a "Top of the Table Member," which means he is in the top 25 percent of all insurance producers, measured by sales in the world. He is also a member of the International Association of Registered Financial Consultants, Inc. He is a past Chairman's Council member for MetLife, Allmerica Financial, Lincoln

Financial, National Life, Penn Mutual Life, John Hancock Life, and Connecticut Mutual Life.

He has long been active in community affairs with the nonprofit organizations Christmas in the City and the Baystate Charitable Foundation.

The author can be reached at hlazarus@baystatefinancial.com

by phone at (617) 585-4510

ACKNOWLEDGMENTS

I have been so fortunate to have the best assistant in the world, Beisy Navarro. She has been with me since 2006, her senior year in high school, and through college, where she graduated with honors. Beisy is now fully licensed for insurance and securities and a junior partner and valuable member of my team with a commitment to the future of my practice.

There are so many people that I would like to thank for their input, in no special order. However, *first and foremost*, I want to thank my wife, Sharon, and my entire family. A very special thanks to my dear friend Paula Witkin for her great command of the English language. Suzy Taylor, from Oxhey, England, the gifted paper-cut artist whose paper-cut has been photographed and licensed for the cover design of my book. Next, Dave Porter, Patricia Annino, Pete Ganley, my dear friend Peter Kaplan, Rabbi Baruch HaLevi, Dr. Evan Longin, Dr. David Danforth, Donna and Vincent Bono, Kathleen and Bob Daly, Jim Ash, Amy and Jason Grover, Marc Diamond, and my longtime friend Constance Hubbell, who have all contributed to this endeavor. I especially want to thank my editor, Linda Cashdan, without whose efforts and talent this book would have not come to fruition.

Most of all I would like to thank all of my wonderful and loyal clients who have made my life feel fulfilled and whose stories make up the bulk of this work.

You should know all of the stories in this book are true. However, some of the names have been changed at the request of a number of the clients and people being interviewed. I want to thank many of the acquaintances and some complete strangers who merely wanted to have someone to speak with and share their life experiences. Because ... *it's all about life.*